THE GRAND OPENING GAME PLAN

SECRETS FROM 100+ GRAND OPENINGS:
STRATEGIES & TACTICS WE LEARNED TO ACQUIRE CUSTOMERS BEFORE LAUNCH

HEATHER CUTLER & KRIS OLIVO

To our team, our clients, other business owners, and future entrepreneurs out there:

Thank you for being *Almost Magical.*

- Kris and Heather

Contents

Chapter 1

Why We Wrote This Book

"When you develop a game plan to get what you want, you will develop a belief that you can get it."

- Zig Ziglar

Most people that want to start a business dream of the same thing. They dream of long lines of eager customers ready to buy their products or services. But in actuality, that isn't what most individuals experience. Almost fifty percent of businesses fail during the first five years.

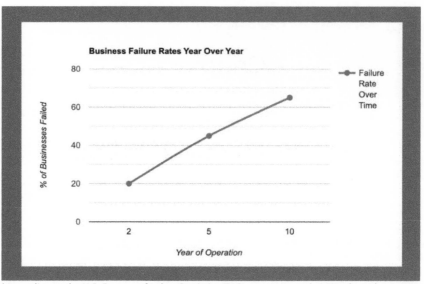

According to the U.S. Bureau of Labor Statistics (BLS), approximately 20% of new businesses fail during the first two years of being open, 45% during the first five years, and 65% during the first 10 years.

Unfortunately, this makes the statistics much more gloomy than encouraging. But that doesn't always have to be the case. The truth is, the odds stack up against your favor. But that's because the playing field isn't always level.

In this book, we're attempting to show you some things that have helped us level the playing field for others. That way, if you're going to play the game of opening a business, you have a great shot at winning from the very start.

Before we start, please do me a favor and imagine something. Think back to all your hard work to get where you are. Think back to all the blood, sweat, tears, and sacrifices you had to make to get here. Reflect on the risks you took yourself. Think about the people who doubted you, the money you saved to invest in your business, and finally start it.

Now, please jump into the future and imagine day one of your business. You open the doors, and a massive flood of customers come crashing through, ready to try your service or product. You feel amazing. Everything is running, and it feels like all that sacrifice has paid off. You feel validated. You are successful. How does that feel? What does it mean to you? Because that's exactly how our client felt when we first helped him open up his business in Las Vegas. We want you to feel the same thing. This book is about how to get massive amounts of customers with a systematic approach. This works even if you've already opened and your grand opening didn't go as well as planned.

Now, if you're like other business owners I know, I can guess what you're feeling now. You're reading this book because you want a successful grand opening.

You might feel overwhelmed by opening a business without having an excellent roadmap. You have a game plan and want to see other things other people have done to succeed with their openings. You may have already opened, felt disappointed because it didn't go as you had hoped, or you've been open for a while. You're struggling with customer acquisition at this point.

If any of those things are true, I want you to keep reading because this book might change your business.

Why did we write this book?

We wrote it to help business owners understand the following:

- How to have a great grand opening.
- The impact of having a great grand opening.
- How to fix a lackluster grand opening.
- The best mindset to have before and after your grand opening for long-term success.

What are you going to get by reading this?

You'll learn how to avoid the disappointment of having a lousy grand opening. We are going to share with you:

- What we've learned after 100+ grand openings.
- Actionable tactics and strategies that we have seen provide the most growth.

- The secrets of an effective grand opening.
- A complete list of digital assets most new business owners should set up.
- How your mindset impacts your results.
- A step-by-step process to fix a grand opening and how one strategy can fix a slump in a business.

Sound like it's worth your time? Then keep reading.

So who are we, and why does any of what we say matter?

We're award-winning marketing agency owners with years of experience opening new businesses. We have helped turn around already-established companies. At the time of writing this book, we've helped thousands of business owners and have done over 100 grand openings.

What this book is and what it isn't.

This book is the game plan we have followed to help our clients be successful. Quick disclaimer: it will not make you successful on its own. Knowledge, unless applied, is useless. Its utility is all in the execution. So how do you execute in the best way? That starts with having a good game plan. This isn't a cheat code that replaces hard work. It is a plan that we have followed to get our clients the results they want.

So if you're ready to learn:

- ☀ The secrets to an effective grand opening.
- ☀ The impact of having a great grand opening.
- ☀ The best mindset for success pre and post-grand opening.
- ☀ How to fix a grand opening or slump in the business.

Keep reading.

Action Step:

1. Write down your "why."

   Having a strong "why" is crucial to enduring the challenges of becoming successful. Why do you want to be successful? What does it mean to you? What changes in your life when you achieve the level of success you've set for yourself? What are the biggest takeaways you are looking to get from this book?

Chapter 2

What We've Learned After 100+ Grand Openings

"Knowledge is power. Information is liberating."

- Kofi Annan

We like to lead with value, so let's start with the main point.

After launching **more than 100 grand openings**, there's a secret we've learned.

We have found a **repeatable and scalable formula for success that anyone can learn.**

And it doesn't matter if your business is brick-and-mortar or online.

If you want massive amounts of customers lining up at your grand opening, this formula can help you.

You can use this same formula to fix poor grand openings that lacked strategy. You can also use this formula to relaunch grand openings that never happened in the first place.

This can seem messy, so **we have broken it down into a digestible, step-by-step process**.

And that's what we're going to teach you in this book.

But first, I want to share a story about one of our clients, we'll call her Laura.

Laura broke the grand opening record in her franchise - twice.

Let's talk about the first one.

Laura was opening a business in Odessa, Texas, when she came to our agency to help plan her grand opening.

In her strategy session, she said, "I want to be the best franchisee in this franchise. I want to have the biggest opening and the most customers."

We love that kind of energy and took it to heart.

So, we followed the formula.

Following the steps in this book, we:

- ☀ Set her up with a foundation for success.
- ☀ Determined who her audience was and where they were consuming content.
- ☀ Crafted an unbeatable offer.
- ☀ Launched ads on social media.
- ☀ Coached her on local marketing practices.

And then we watched the appointments pour in.

Foundation –> Audience –> Offer –> Advertise –> Local Grassroots = Appointments

On Grand Opening Day, she and her team executed **a record of 101 services in a single day**.

The previous single-day franchise record was **87 services**.

Over the Grand Opening Weekend (Saturday and Sunday), she totaled **163 services**.

That's how you want to launch a business - with a tidal wave, not a splash.

Another client, we'll call him Jonathan, opened his business in Lakeland, Florida. He asked us for help launching his grand opening.

We followed the formula, and his location performed **192 services in a 3-day grand opening**.

Again - tidal wave.

Let's pivot back to Laura for the grand opening of her second location.

We launched the same offer and processes in her new location in Midland, Texas.

Her team performed 123 services on Grand Opening Day **to beat the franchise record again**.

When we say there is a method to the grand opening madness, we mean it, and anyone can learn it.

In the following chapters, **we will outline the steps you can take to find this same success**.

Each step plays a vital role in the success of your launch - **there is no fluff in this book**.

Failing to dial in each step can water down the outcome. Why?

Because consumer purchasing behavior is predictable. **If you can give the right offer, to the right person, at the right time, you have a high chance of getting the customer to buy.**

Right Offer + Right Person + Right Time = High Chance of Conversion

The steps we will share with you create controllable outcomes and scalability.

Keep in mind that there is a right and wrong way to do this. But, like Uncle Ben in Spider-Man said, "with great power comes great responsibility."

Our Grand Opening Game Plan is powerful but can also cause damage when executed poorly. Especially when planning the first impression a customer will have of your business. We'll talk more about that in later chapters.

If you follow the steps we are about to lay out, it will be unreasonable for you not to gain traction in your market.

Keep reading to learn more about the road you're about to travel down that leads to grand opening success.

Action Step:

1. Start to brainstorm and write down all of your ideas for your grand opening. The idea here is to get all your ideas on paper so you analyze them more thoroughly as we discuss strategies and tactics in the coming chapters.

Chapter 3

What This Will Cover & Who This Is For

"Whether you think you can, or think you can't -- you're right."

– Henry Ford

Let's be honest; no one likes their time wasted. So to ensure we're not wasting your time, let's agree on something.

Advice is only valuable and practical when you deliver it in the proper context. The situation, the audience, and the timing matter.

Good advice + the right audience + the right timing = Practical value

How do you know this book is for you and not wasting your time?

This book is for you if you're opening a business and want a great grand opening.

This book is for you if you've already opened a business and want to get more customers in one massive land grab.

This book is for you if you've already opened and it didn't go as well as planned.

This book is for you if you're a seasoned entrepreneur starting something new in unfamiliar territory.

Finally, this book is for you if you bought a business that is already open and needs a fresh relaunch to turn it around.

Do any of those situations sound familiar? If you said yes, let's keep moving.

Now that you know this is for you, you may think, "What actual value am I going to receive from this book?"

We are going to cover all the tactics, systems, strategies, and approaches we have taken to help our clients have crazy successful openings.

Keep reading because we're about to unveil the secrets of our game plan and what has worked for us in the field.

First, there is something we want you to keep in mind. **Knowing the impact of something is essential to having the motivation to do it.** But before we discuss why all the steps we're about to show you matter, let's go over some marketing terms you need to know.

Action Steps:

1. Think about a time when you received good advice, but the timing was off, or think about a time when you gave good advice but someone didn't take it.

2. What were the roadblocks you or someone else encountered that prevented the execution of that advice?

Chapter 4

Marketing Words You Should Know

"Learning is a treasure that will follow its owner everywhere."

- Chinese Proverb

Let's be clear; we don't want to overwhelm you with fancy terminology. But, to understand everything we are talking about, we must speak the same language. So here are some of the words you should know. You can reference this chapter as needed.

Impression - the number of times an ad or post is shown.

Cost Per Thousand (CPM) - is used to denote the price of 1,000 advertisement impressions on an advertisement.

Reach - the number of people an ad or post is shown to.

Engagement - refers to people engaging on your page or posts by liking, clicking, commenting, sharing, or reacting to your posts.

Cost Per Result (CPR) - the cost it takes to get a particular outcome from your advertisement. This can be a click, a booked appointment, a landing page view, etc. CPR varies depending on what your goal is when it comes to your advertising campaign.

Organic - means a non-paid post. An example of this is a regular social media post you didn't pay to post. That's an organic post.

Non-Organic - means a paid post. An example of this could be a boosted post or an advertisement on Facebook,

Instagram, TikTok, etc. Those ads are considered non-organic posts.

Search Engine Optimization (SEO) - the process of improving how well you appear in search results.

Cost Per Acquisition (CPA) - the cost it takes to get a customer.

Lifetime Value (LTV) - the total value a customer has to your business over the lifetime of them buying from you.

Your CPA and LTV are two of the most critical metrics to understand when you're operating your business. This ensures that you're acquiring customers at a profitable margin. So let's dive a little further into this.

Imagine if it takes you $100 to get a customer, and their LTV is $10.

This wouldn't be a good scenario because, typically, you want a lower CPA than the LTV of a particular customer. Otherwise, it is not a profitable scenario. This is critical because if you're not profitably growing, then it's tough to sustain a business.

So let's look at the last example reversed. Imagine the CPA of that customer is $10, but the LTV of that customer is $100. This means you're making money with each customer you get, and you can spend as much as you can handle at scale to get customers. **When you're getting a return on your advertising,**

it's easy to scale your budget. If you can scale your budget, you can outspend your competitors. If you can outspend your competitors, you can dominate your market.

Ultimately the job of a business is not just to make money but to make a profit. Chances are, if you're reading this, you didn't go into business not to make money, right? So knowing your LTV and CPA are very important for you to understand to grow your business as large as you'd like it to be. We could spend more time on this topic, but a deep dive into unit economics is beyond the scope of this book.

But, you should get exposure to these concepts.

Now that we've covered some of those terms, let's talk about the impact of a successful grand opening.

Action Step:

1. Study the above terms and quiz yourself on their definitions. The more you understand these terms, the better you can understand your business and marketing effectiveness.

Chapter 5

The Impact of A Great Grand Opening

"The result of long-term relationships is better and better quality and lower and lower costs."

- W. Edwards Deming

The grand opening of your business can yield a lot of positive results. **But only if you create a game plan to squeeze the most juice out of it.**

You want to be proactive, not reactive.

A great grand opening can determine how well you do in your business's first six to twelve months and impacts the following:

- Your viral coefficient (we'll explain this later)
- Your customer list
- Reviews and testimonials
- The amount of user-generated content created
- How much FOMO you generate
- Data available to be used in later advertising

So, let us ask you a question.

Have you ever referred a friend or family member to a business?

You most likely have.

But why?

You may have felt the urge to share because you had a fantastic experience and wanted others to know.

Creating the urge to share an experience is the most important effect of a grand opening. We want to provide a memorable experience worthy of sharing with others.

Creating an experience worthy of sharing with others is how you get your business to "go viral."

Having a viral business **is how you get more people to become customers without having to pay to acquire them**.

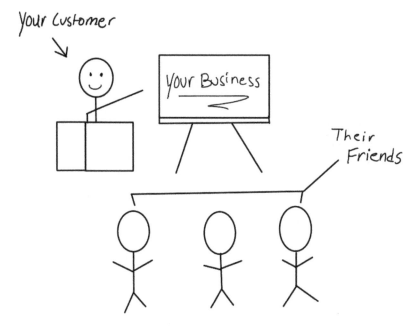

Let us explain.

THE 'VIRAL COEFFICIENT'

Let's pretend you purchased from a business. Afterward, you shared your positive experience with three other people. Of those three people, two of them buy from that business.

Those two people became new customers and required zero acquisition costs. This happened by word of mouth.

Then, those two customers tell eight people about their positive experiences. Of those eight people, three of them buy from the business.

This goes on and on.

This is an example of a 'viral coefficient.'

A viral coefficient is the number of new customers generated by existing customers. **This is how a company can achieve exponential customer growth**.

The good news is that this isn't just a theory.

You can calculate the actual viral coefficient of your business with this formula:

$$\frac{\text{\# of Customers You Have} \times \text{\# of Referrals Each Customer Produces} \times \text{Average Conversion Rate for Referrals}}{\text{\# of Customers You Have}}$$

Multiply the <number of customers you have> X <number of referrals each customer produces> X <average conversion rate for referrals> and then divide that number by <the number of customers you have>.

The number you get after solving this formula is your viral coefficient.

Here's an example:

$$\frac{500 \times 4 \times 30\%}{500} = 1.2$$

500 would be the number of customers the business has.

4 is the number of referrals each customer generates.

30% is the average conversion rate for referrals.

1.2 would be the viral coefficient.

> **A viral coefficient greater than 1 means a business can grow without relying only on paid marketing.**
>
> **This is because new customers will share your business with others, and a percentage of those people will become customers for free.**

The larger your viral coefficient (for example, 1.2, 1.5, 1.75, 2.5, etc.), the more exponential your growth can be. This is because the Customer Acquisition Cost (CAC) will decrease over time.

If you have a Viral Coefficient of 2.5, that means that for every customer you acquire, that customer brings in 2.5 more customers.

> You cannot buy a high viral coefficient. Its growth is directly correlated to the quality of your product or service and whether people naturally want to share it.

If you have a quality product or service that people want to share, you can get a high viral coefficient. If you don't, then people will not share your business.

This is why having a great grand opening with a five-star experience is so important. We need customers to share their experiences with others.

BUILD AND OWN YOUR CUSTOMER LIST (NOT A THIRD-PARTY COMPANY)

> Building a customer list you own is one of the most important things you can do as a business owner.

Now, before you sum this up to "getting contact information," hear us out about why this is so important.

You can't control third-party platforms like Facebook.

- ☀ Paid advertising costs can fluctuate.
- ☀ The platform could become less popular.
- ☀ The platform can get hacked.
- ☀ The platform can get shut down or sold.
- ☀ You could be kicked off the platform.

You're risking your customer list if you rely on third-party platforms to build up and store your customer's information.

When you own your list of customers and their information, no one can take it from you. It becomes something you can turn to anytime you need to push sales.

List Ownership = Security

During your grand opening, collect information that will help with future marketing. This can include names, emails, phone numbers, birthdays, and other relevant information. You can also use this information to create customized experiences later.

It's best practice to store this information somewhere easily accessible. This can be a CRM (client relationship management software), POS, or spreadsheet. The big thing here is to make sure that you have a backup somewhere, regardless of where it's stored.

Now let's talk about reviews.

REVIEWS & TESTIMONIALS

What does almost every person do before they make a purchasing decision?

They check reviews.

Why?

Because human purchasing behavior doesn't always trust paid advertising.

We all know a company will say good things about its own product or service. Consumers want to know another customer's experience before they assume the risk of buying.

Amazon is an easy example of this.

When you select a product to buy on Amazon, the page will show how many reviews the product has and the average number of stars the product is rated.

The barrier to purchasing lowers when a buyer sees thousands of five-star reviews and an average positive rating. This lets the prospective buyer know that this is a safe purchase. Humans do this with even the most minor purchasing decisions, such as buying a new phone charger. The importance of generating positive reviews can't be understated, and there is no better time to gain plenty of positive reviews than during your grand opening.

Reviews also help increase your online authority and help your organic SEO (search engine optimization). This is because search engines want to provide the best result for users when they are searching. So if it has the choice to display a product with one review versus 100, it will typically choose the one with 100 because it seems more credible.

One thing to note is that you want to ensure you respond to every single review - good or bad. This lets the search engines know that you care about your customers and are very active, which boosts your ranking. Responding to every review also lets your customers know you care about their experience. This can be especially critical when customers see how you respond to a negative review. An empathetic response to a negative review can sway the person who left it to change it and soften its impact on other prospective customers.

THE EFFECT OF NEGATIVE CUSTOMER EXPERIENCES

A customer with a bad business experience will tell other people about it — every time.

We don't have to look further than our own consumer behavior to confirm this.

Think about your purchasing habits.

There are probably several businesses you like and buy from often, **but you haven't left them a review yet**.

But, if you've had a poor customer experience, we're willing to bet you didn't keep it to yourself. Instead, you may have left a negative review and told others about it.

Businesses often don't realize how negative experiences and reviews can hurt their business. And it usually happens faster than you'd expect. However, we'll cover more on this in a later chapter.

Now let's get into user-generated content.

USER-GENERATED CONTENT

We want your customers to post about your product or service on their social media channels.

When your customers do this, it's called User-Generated Content (UGC).

> **When we get customers to post about our business on their social media channels, our business is seen by their audience for free.**

Because a customer, not the business, created and shared the content, that content becomes another form of social proof.

UGC is extremely powerful. Think about this in your own life. Has a friend ever posted about a restaurant, and their post made you want to try it out? That is the power of UGC.

FOMO (FEAR OF MISSING OUT)

The offer around your grand opening should trigger customers to take action sooner than they would otherwise.

They should feel excited, but more importantly, **they should fear missing out on a great opportunity**.

Fear is an excellent motivator in marketing - **use it responsibly**.

We create this feeling in many ways. You can craft an offer that's so good the customer would feel dumb saying no to it. Many variables go into this, such as the features, bonuses, attractions, scarcity, and urgency, but we'll cover this later in the book when we discuss creating your "FOMOGO offer".

ADVERTISING DATA FOR LATER ADVERTISING

When you run paid advertisements online, the ads will collect and store data from your potential customers.

Now, **not all the people targeted with your advertising will show up to the grand opening. So, it is important that we use the already-collected data in future advertisements**.

This is how we show more ads to people after the grand opening to convert them.

Later in this book, we'll get into how this relates to the money spent on your advertising (ad spend) and your overall costs.

But one of the positive effects of your grand opening advertising is the influx of data you will get that you can leverage later.

We've discussed the effects of having a great grand opening. But now we need to discuss how to formulate your grand opening game plan.

To do that, we need to determine which field your business is playing on; keep reading to find out how customer acquisition has changed.

Action Steps:
1. Write down a business you frequently refer others to.
2. Write what makes you share that brand as often as you do.
3. Write down what you like about them and what you tend to share about them.
4. After you've done that, write down why you think someone would want to share your business.

The points you write down can help you later in crafting your advertising and when speaking to people about your business.

Chapter 6

How Customer Acquisition Has Changed

"The average attention span of the modern human being is about half as long as whatever you're trying to tell them."

- Meg Rosoff

What do a goldfish and a human have in common?

They have similar attention spans.

Over the last 20 years, the average human attention span has shrunk significantly.

This is mostly due to technology becoming more integrated into our daily lives.

Because we have developed a more intimate relationship with technology, there's far more competition for our attention than ever.

As a result of this shift, if you're a business that wants to succeed long-term, **your business has to go from "what's this brand I heard about?" to "what's this brand I keep hearing about?"**

The ideology, "build a business and people will come" does not work anymore with most companies.

I mean, think about it.

> **Just because you build something doesn't mean anyone knows about it.**

According to a 2015 report by Microsoft, the average human attention span decreased from 12 seconds to 8 seconds since the year 2000. This was approximately when mobile devices became more mainstream.

In fact, most marketing agencies know that the majority of people don't make it past three to four seconds when looking at media. This is because there are far more distractions and businesses competing for our attention now than before.

We see advertisements every time we use social media.

The podcasts we listen to have ads.

There are advertisements at the gas station and billboards everywhere we look.

You can't even go to the bathroom at a bar without seeing an ad.

Even Amazon's Alexa has suggestions and advertises to us in our homes.

There are so many things that distract us that we can't help but lose attention. Unfortunately, this makes staying focused difficult for most people.

Let's talk about how this affects advertising.

When someone sees an ad and takes action, usually, it's not the first time that person has seen an ad from that company.

You can see this in your own life. When was the last time you saw a new advertisement and immediately took action?

Most of the time that doesn't happen.

On average, a consumer experiences many impressions before they take action. Impressions are the number of times your content is displayed, whether clicked or not.

Knowing this is key. There's a reason why Coca-Cola still advertises. It's because they want to stay top of mind with their consumers. That way, when you start craving a soda, you're more likely to think of Coke than another brand.

How many impressions should a brand push out? As many as necessary.

In our company's early days, we set the bar at eight impressions before we expected meaningful engagement. Now we shoot for 20.

So let's play out what this scenario might look like.

The first time someone looks at an ad, they don't see it. They keep scrolling.

The second time, they see it but don't notice it.

The third time, the person becomes aware of it being there.

The fourth time, the person somewhat remembers seeing it at one point or another.

The fifth time, they look at the picture or video and keep moving.

The sixth time, they read what the advertisement says.

The seventh time, they reread it and continued with their day.

The eighth time, they think, "there's that ad again."

The ninth time, they started to take more interest in it.

The tenth time, they look at the ad's comments and see what people say.

The eleventh time, they wonder if they want the product/service.

The twelfth time, they look at everything again with more scrutiny.

The thirteenth time, they think, "hmm, I might want this."

The fourteenth time, they start justifying why they need it and what use it would have in their life.

The fifteenth time, they check the price.

The sixteenth time, they think, maybe I'll buy this one day.

The seventeenth time, they checked the company's credibility.

The eighteenth time, they think that maybe they shouldn't.

The nineteenth time, they decide they probably should, and they check out if there are any deals.

The twentieth time they see the ad, they buy it.

Prospect Ad Awareness Journey Map

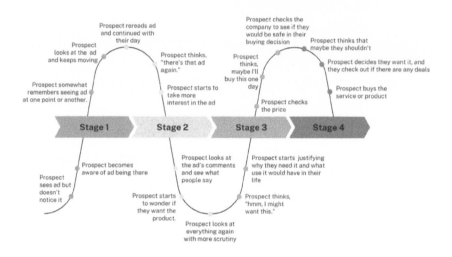

Long journey, right? This is because of the rise of digital marketing.

Companies have a more intimate and immediate level of interaction with their customers.

Before digital marketing, you could do direct mail advertisements. But when you think about it, most people aren't obsessing over the stack of coupons, postcards, and advertisements left in their mailboxes daily. Most times, they head straight to the trash bin.

You could do TV advertisements, which were and still are very expensive for most small businesses.

Radio ads have a similar situation.

Smartphones and social media changed everything. People started spending unprecedented amounts of time on their phones due to the addicting nature of social media. Social media platforms designed this addictiveness to monetize that attention via ads because using the platform is free. They needed the platforms to be free so people would join. That is their model. They sell our attention.

Think about the average person's day.

They wake up, and they check their phone. They scroll on their social platforms.

They see ad after ad while they're scrolling.

They go to work.

On their way, they may listen to a podcast with advertisements in it.

They stop to get gas and see ads at the pump.

They finally get to work, and in every free minute they have, they're checking their phone. What do they see?

More ads competing for their attention.

According to a study by Slick Text, the average mobile phone user checks their phone up to 63 times a day. Pretty astonishing.

This all shows the level of addiction we have to our devices, which is why companies need to advertise on them. **It's where the attention is**.

Another 2019 study by Provision Living, reported the average American spends an average screen time of 5.4 hours on their mobile phones daily.

This is a significant chunk of someone's day.

So, for a company to stay top of mind, they must do what we discussed earlier. Customers have to go from, "what is this brand I heard about?" to "what's this brand I keep hearing about?"

Suppose a consumer sees an ad for your business at 9 a.m. By 9 p.m. that evening, they have likely seen an additional 62 ads, plus social media posts from their friends. What do you think they will remember? Your initial ad from 12 hours ago? Probably not.

Understanding this journey and its obstacles is critical in marketing your business effectively.

> **You have to know the playing field you're playing on to win the game.**

This mentality is often seen in sports and war.

It's common for track athletes to walk the track they're going to compete on before running their race. That way, they know how to navigate the course, which increases their chance of winning.

Generals will look at the terrain they are fighting on to be more effective.

Cliff jumpers will survey their landing zone and water before jumping. The list goes on and on.

The lesson here is: always study the field you're playing on. This preparation can help increase your chance of success in any effort.

So now that you know the playing field, keep reading, and let's talk about how to win the actual game.

Action Steps:

1. Make a list of all the places where your ideal customer is spending their time. This way, you will have an idea of where your advertisements should be placed.

2. Think about other brands similar to your own. How often do you see their advertising? Where do you see it? What do they advertise?

Chapter 7

Step 1: Structuring for Success

"You can't build a great building on a weak foundation. You must have a solid foundation if you're going to have a strong superstructure."

- Gordon B. Hinckley

Let's say you're trying to build a castle; this castle is your business.

In this scenario, you want your castle to be big because who wants a small castle?

The entrance should have a flag so that everyone can see your branding.

You want it to be well-organized so that your operations run smoothly.

It should have tall walls and a moat so potential enemies (hackers) can't break into it.

Your castle can only be this strong if it sits on a solid foundation. That's what we'll talk about in this chapter: how to build the foundation of your business.

We'll talk about the accounts you need, how to get started, and how to protect what you build.

The reason why we wrote this chapter is that **a lot of business owners get stuck here**. They overthink the process and ask themselves, "Should I be on Facebook? What about Twitter? Do I need a website?"

There are a ton of options to consider, which can cause inaction. The reality is you'll want to get these set up quickly so you can move on to acquiring customers.

To make this easy, we've listed the necessary accounts, platforms, and assets you need to be visible online.

This list might not include every asset your specific business needs, but we find the following applies to almost everyone.

Let's get started.

BUY YOUR DOMAIN

A domain is what a customer types into an internet browser to search for a website. For example, Google's domain is 'google.com.'

Buy a domain that matches the name of your business. For example, if the name of your business is 'I Love Dogs,' you would want to buy 'ilovedogs.com' if it's available and affordable.

We recommend buying a few other variations of your domain, like 'ilikedogs.com' or 'ilovedoggos.com.'

You want to do this because your competitors could buy these variations to trick people into finding their business instead of yours. We've seen this happen to other companies first-hand.

Buying domains through companies like GoDaddy or NameCheap is easy and usually inexpensive. The domain typically renews yearly, so account for that in your expenses.

WEBSITE

Yes, you need one; but no, it doesn't have to be complicated.

Having a website acts as a catch-all from every other platform we will mention moving forward. For example, when customers hear about you on Facebook, they'll likely go to your website to learn more.

When you build your website, **focus on posting the essential information and then move on**. You can always add more pages and details to your website when you have time and bandwidth. For now, the basic details will do.

You can hire someone to help build your website or do it yourself. There are a ton of drag-and-drop website builders that are incredibly user-friendly.

Website builders are constantly growing and changing. A few prominent companies now include Wix, Squarespace, and Shopify.

Keep in mind that you will pay a fee to host your website. That means the platform you choose to build your website will charge you a monthly fee to keep the website live.

Once you've built your website, you'll connect the domain you purchased to the website to make it searchable.

There are extensive tutorials on how to do this on YouTube and the platform your choose.

SOCIAL MEDIA

Think of this section as claiming your digital real estate online. Will you be active on every single one of these platforms moving forward?

Probably not.

But you want to create an account on as many relevant platforms as possible. Upload your logo, link to your website, and list all your business details. There are two reasons why: **Securing your account**. Someone else might take it if you don't own your account on the platform.

- ☀ **Creating an account on each platform makes your business more visible**. This helps potential customers find you on their platform of choice.

Below is a list of all the currently relevant social media platforms you should create an account on. Add others as necessary:

- ⚐ Facebook
  - Do you have a personal Facebook account? If not, create that first. Facebook requires all business pages to be created by a personal account. There is no way around this. Your business page won't show content from your personal page and vice versa. This is just the structure Facebook mandates. A business page is always connected to a personal account.
  - Go to 'business.facebook.com' and create a Business Manager account. Once you've made your Business Manager account, you can create your business page.

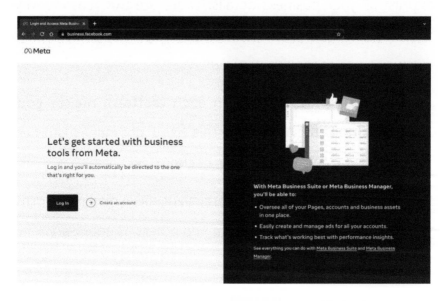

- It is against the terms and conditions of Facebook to create more than one personal account. Doing so can get you restricted, so please do not do that.

☀ Instagram

Tip: When you sign up for your account, use an accessible cell phone number instead of an email. The deliverability of Instagram's account recovery emails can be unreliable, but a phone number usually works. When you create the account, it will default to a 'personal' account. Switch to a 'professional' account in the account's settings or under 'edit profile'. Doing so maximizes advertising features and allows the account to connect to your business's Facebook page.

Cancel　　　　　**Edit profile**　　　　Done

Change profile photo

Name	Grand Opening Game Plan 🏆
Username	grandopeninggameplan
Website	http://grandopeninggameplan.com
Bio	Grandopeninggameplan.com

Switch to professional account

Create avatar

Personal information settings

- ☀ LinkedIn
  - Yes, you should have a personal LinkedIn account as a business owner and a separate LinkedIn account for your business.
- ☀ TikTok
  - As with Instagram, you want to change from a 'Personal' account to a 'Professional' account.
- ☀ Pinterest
- ☀ YouTube
- ☀ Twitter

Getting the exact account name or 'handle' for each account is wise so you are consistent across the board. In keeping with our last example, your company's handle would be @ilovedogs on all platforms.

GOOGLE MY BUSINESS (GMB)

Create your account at: www.google.com/business

Google My Business creates a business profile on Google, so your information shows up when someone searches for your business.

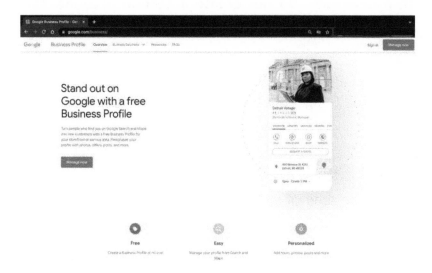

You have probably seen these listings when you've used Google to search for a business near you. **It lists the name of your business, website, address, and hours of operation. It also lists options to book an appointment or buy a product**. You can upload photos of your business or products, and it's where customers can leave reviews. It is also how people can find you on Google Maps.

It is effortless to create and maintain this account. Doing so helps your SEO, and we recommend replying to every review because it helps your business look active online.

Google will send you a postcard in the mail to confirm your business's address. The postcard will contain a verification code that is **only valid for five days**. If you miss receiving the postcard and the five days expire, you must apply for another postcard with a new code. **Do not create a second account**. This is known as a 'duplicate' account and can cause issues down the road.

Create your Google My Business account when you have the keys to your mailbox. This will help ensure you don't miss the postcard.

Note: At the time of writing this, Google does not accept PO boxes as a valid address to send the verification postcard. If you operate an online business out of your home and want to get on Google Maps, you must list your home address or another physical address.

APPLE MAPS

Create your account at: register.apple.com/placesonmaps

Listing your business on Apple Maps is easy. Like Google My Business, you will add your business's details to complete your profile. Unlike Google My Business, Apple Maps allows you to answer the phone at your business or upload specific documents to verify your account.

YELP

Create your account, populate it with your information, and respond to reviews.

EMAIL AND PHONE NUMBER

There are many places to create a business email, but we have found Google is one of the easiest and most reliable.

Go to 'workspace.google.com' to create an admin console for your business on Google. This is where you will integrate your domain to create emails for your company like 'hello@ilovedogs.com' or 'support@ilovedogs.com.'

There is a fee to create and host the emails you'll make. **But sending emails from your business email is more professional than using a free Gmail**.

That said, we also recommend claiming your free Gmail account for your business, such as ilovedogs@gmail.com, so no one else can take it.

If you are struggling to do this, many videos on YouTube show you step-by-step instructions.

We also recommend buying a dedicated business phone number instead of using a personal cell phone number.

Leading up to your grand opening, you may not have anyone at your business to answer the phone. Ensure you use tools like voicemail and call forwarding to respond to your customers.

LOGO

This is probably already done for you if you are part of a franchise. But, if you are not part of a franchise, you will likely need to get a logo made.

You can easily make a logo with free programs like Canva. You can also pay someone to create a logo by finding a graphic designer on platforms like Fiverr.com.

Whether you already have a logo or you need to design one from scratch, **here is a list of file types you will want to get. This helps so you can apply the correct file type to any situation**:

If you can, ask for the source files. Source Files are the files used to create the logo in its rawest form. Usually, this is going to be an Adobe Illustrator or Photoshop file. Many times, a creator may charge more for these files, but we recommend paying to get them. This is helpful if you are ever doing large print graphics.

- JPEG (white background, black background)
- Transparent PNG (no background)
- PDF (print-only file type)
- Large and small file sizes
- At least one logo with white space around all the edges of your logo. **This helps ensure your logo is not cut off when you upload it to a circular frame** (like an Instagram profile photo).

Over time, you will need to upload your logo online and print it for various purposes. **Having appropriate file sizes ensures your logo always looks clean and never pixelated**.

TWO-FACTOR AUTHENTICATION

This is **one of the most critical steps**, so don't skip over it.

Turn on two-factor authentication on every platform we listed above.

Doing so is the number one thing you can do to stop hackers from gaining access to your accounts. Unfortunately, hackers and scammers are more prevalent and relentless than ever. So you want to make sure you do this.

Two-factor authentication is an extra step required by a platform to verify that the person logging in to the account owns it. Usually, this is a verification code sent to a phone number.

Sometimes people do not like to turn on two-factor authentication because it takes a little longer to access the account. We understand. But we'd also argue that getting your account hacked is worse.

We'll share some real-life examples at the end of the chapter, but please ensure you do this on every account you can.

A NOTE ON SECURITY

When you start a business and sign up for different accounts, your online information will become more easily available.

As a result, it isn't hard for hackers to find your information and try to get personal information from you. This comes in many forms. It could be a text message, email, or notification that prompts you to click a link for a fake reason.

If you click the link, the hackers can break into your account, steal your credit card information, and even take your entire account hostage.

> **This is very preventable. Be aware of messages you receive, and do not click on anything you are unsure of.**

For example, Facebook will never text you to tell you your ad account has been suspended, but that is a common trick hackers use.

If you get an email saying your account has been suspended, look at who sent the email. To do this, look at the information after the '@' in the 'From' email address. Many hackers often have an email that looks fake such as 'nick@3847498domain23.com' but claims to be from Facebook.

These are not authentic emails from a business. If you get something like this, do not click on anything. Instead, log into the existing account to investigate for yourself.

When in doubt, do not click on anything irregularly sent to you. Always log in to your original account from a clean browser window to see if the claim is valid.

In our agency, a client clicked a link they shouldn't have and had their entire account taken hostage. The hackers gained access to the client's Facebook Business Manager in this instance. They removed all the admins, made themselves admins, gained access to the Ads Manager, **and charged over $900 to the credit card on file**.

This may surprise some of you, but Facebook's Support is not always responsive. It took over six months for this situation to be rectified.

Please, be aware of anything sent to you.

DO NOT LET A MARKETING AGENCY SET UP ACCOUNTS FOR YOU

Like the savvy business owner you are, you might think it would be a good idea to hire a marketing agency to set all of this up for you. While we agree that hiring an agency is extremely helpful, beware of any agency that offers to create these accounts for you using their information (email, etc.).

> **If you allow another agency to create your accounts, they will own the accounts and the data - not you.**

At our agency, we provide a 60-90 minute onboarding session with every new client. During this call, we ask the client to share their computer screen while we walk them through the account creation process. **Then, we give our agency access. Our clients own their assets, not us**.

Morally, we believe this is the right thing to do. You should have complete control over your assets and data as a business owner. If you don't, you are at the mercy of the morals of that agency.

Early in our agency, a client came to us to run ads on Facebook. This client had been working with another agency that created their Facebook page. The agency still had ownership of the page.

We emailed the agency many times, asking them to transfer the Facebook page over to our client. The agency never responded and never turned over the Facebook page.

After many attempts to get the page back through Facebook Support, we were forced to start over from scratch and make a new page. **The client had to rebuild all the likes, followers, reviews, etc. It was all lost.**

If a marketing agency insists on creating the accounts on your behalf, politely ask that they either:

- Create the accounts with your information or
- Walk you through setting up the account and then provide their agency access.

If they refuse to do this - find another agency.

That's it!

Now you have a strong foundation for your business. You're ready to start attracting the right attention from your ideal customers.

Keep reading to learn how.

<u>Action Steps:</u>

1. Buy your domain at namecheap.com or a similar service.
2. Create your social media profiles on every applicable platform and secure your handles.
3. Create your Google My Business listing and start the verification process.
4. Create your Yelp listing.
5. Turn on two-factor authentication for the platforms you use.
6. Create your business email address.
7. Work on creating your logo (if applicable).
8. Hire someone to create your website or sign up for a free account with a website builder and start working on it yourself.
9. Write down all of your logins and passwords on a Google sheet.

Chapter 8

Step 2: Audience & Attention

"If you want to create messages that resonate with your audience, you need to know what they care about."

- Nate Elliot

Imagine a business owner in the middle of the street with a megaphone trying to sell dog food to anyone around. How effective do you think he might be?

If the people walking buy are cat owners, he won't make any sales and he will have wasted time and money advertising to people who are not his ideal customer.

Suppose all the people walking by are dog owners who just ran out of dog food. In that case, the business owner's strategy could be very effective.

But, it's more likely that most people walking by don't fit that criteria.

Knowing who your customers are and where they spend their time is crucial to effective marketing. So before sending your message out to the masses, you want to set up the ideal profile of your customer. That way, you can create the perfect message to attract that customer. Anything less than that will result in spending more money on irrelevant attention.

Keeping that in mind, who would you rather be? The business owner in the street screaming at random people trying to sell dog food, or the person at a convention for dog lovers selling the same product? We're willing to bet the second person will be much more successful.

Knowing and outlining whom you want to get the attention of ensures you attract the right people. You can do this by setting up your consumer demographic or customer avatar. This way, you can craft specific messaging.

That process ensures you're not wasting effort, time, and money on people that don't care about what you sell.

This process is targeted marketing. But to be targeted, you must know whom you're targeting. So what are the steps to do this?

First, start off brainstorming. You want to imagine your ideal customer. Here are some questions to help you narrow this down:

What are the characteristics of my target audience?

What are their ages?

What is their gender?

What is their job title?

What are their income, educational level, and family status?

What motivates my audience?

Where does my customer live?

What are their attitudes and opinions?

What is their political affiliation?

What's the geographic radius that I'm targeting?

Are there specific zip codes? Do I want to go beyond that?

What is their lifestyle?

What are some of their goals?

What are their pain points?

What are their habits?

What do they value?

What are their interests or hobbies?

Which platforms do they enjoy? Is it LinkedIn? Do they spend more time on Instagram? Pinterest? Facebook? TikTok? YouTube?

What type of messaging engages them?

Do they have a specific lingo they use?

How does your target audience interact with a business like yours?

What products and services does your target audience buy?

What kind of purchasing journey matters to your audience?

What type of advertising does your audience consume?

What type of content does your ideal customer want?

What are their fears?

These are questions you want to dive deep into. Why? Because the more you get to know your customer, the better you can attract that customer.

So don't read the questions and not take action. Instead, break out your computer or a notebook and answer them. The little bit of work is worth it. We promise.

Working on your consumer demographic to this level of detail will reduce your churn.

Churn is the percentage rate at which customers leave your business.

You'll be able to target and get their attention much better than you would if you hadn't done this.

No one wants to be the guy screaming in the street to random people.

Okay so now what? You've got a clear picture in mind. Now, it's time to choose the platforms where you intend to focus your advertising efforts.

Depending on your budget and demographic, this can be one platform or many. For most small businesses, we recommend two to three.

Out of those 2 or 3, we recommend that Google be one of those platforms. The reason being is that people are problem-aware when they're searching on Google. So think about the nature of the platform when you're deciding.

People on Google are searching for a solution. That means they know they have a problem already. In contrast, other platforms may be more disruptive-based advertising.

Disruptive-based advertising is showing someone an ad when they aren't looking to solve a problem.

You are disrupting what they are doing.

But, that person could meet the specific selection criteria you have already outlined. Because they meet that criteria, you want to show them an ad. This is how it works.

Facebook is a prime example of this. You can get very detailed with the targeting on Facebook. It is interest-based, meaning you can target people based on their interests. You can use demographics as well.

Facebook also allows you to drill down to a granular level. For example, you could target a mother interested in 'Baby Gap' who lives in a specific area and does not like X. X is an example of a particular thing. It can get pretty precise.

Don't skip over this. When setting up your ideal target audience, you want to think about these options. Explore the platforms to see what they offer when it comes to targeting. Here are some more examples to drive this point home further.

Imagine you sell shirts that say, "I love my Labrador."

Would it make sense to run an ad for people who have cats?

OR

Would an ad for people identified as Labrador owners make more sense?

One of those options has a shot of making you a lot more money than the other.

Here's another example. Let's assume you have baseball cards for sale. Would you try to sell them to someone who only collected stamps?

Are you picking up what we're putting down here?

In summary, using the right message for the right person on the right platform is critical to success.

Right Message + Right Person + Right Platform = Higher Success Rate

What's next? You've done those exercises. We know our target audience and where they are. Keep reading to learn how to give them a grand opening offer so good that they'll feel silly saying no to you.

We call this the FOMOGO offer.

Action Step:

1. Get to know your customer by creating a customer avatar. To do this, write down all the answers to the above bolded questions and any others you may think of.

Chapter 9

Step 3: The FOMOGO Offer

"Make people an offer so good they would feel stupid saying no."

- Travis Jones

We can summarize this chapter in one statement: **Create an offer so valuable the customer would feel like they can't pass it up**.

That's it.

For grand openings we call this the "Fear Of Missing Out Grand Opening Offer" or "FOMOGO Offer" for short.

But before we dive into how you craft an offer like this, we need to talk about mindset, trust, and human purchasing behavior.

We'll apply the term 'barrier to purchase' to this conversation. **A 'barrier to purchase' means any obstacle the customer might encounter and have to overcome to buy**.

There are two types of barriers: technical and mindset.

Technical barriers are easy to solve. It means ensuring the mechanical pathway from viewing the offer to purchasing the product is seamless.

Basically, all the buttons work, and they all do what they're supposed to do.

An example of this would be: a customer views the ad on social media and clicks the button.

Next, the customer is directed to a website featuring that product. From there, they add the product to their cart and pay.

Afterward, a confirmation email is sent to the customer. Of course, if there were a technical issue in any part of this flow, the customer would not be able to buy.

Mechanical Purchase Flow

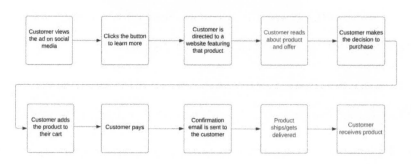

Overcoming 'mindset barriers to purchasing' takes a little more work and understanding of human purchasing behavior.

> **Unless you bought into a well-known franchise, there will likely be some trust your business will initially lack with the customer. This is because they don't know you and have never experienced your service or product.**

Another phrase we need to add to this conversation is the number of 'touches' it takes to get a person to become a paying customer.

A 'touch' in marketing is an instance in which a potential customer sees your brand. For example, a 'touch' can be an ad

72

on Facebook, an organic post on Instagram, a reel on TikTok, an email, a piece of direct mail, viewing a billboard, etc.

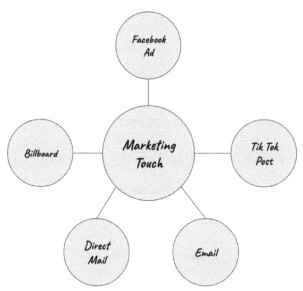

Note: This graph does not represent all possible touch points.

There is an ongoing conversation in marketing about how many brand 'touches' it takes to get a person to become a paying customer. Some experts say the average number of touches required from a brand is between 5-8, and others say it is as high as 20.

Thus, the effectiveness of your marketing will correlate to how many touches it takes for your brand to acquire a customer.

A strong offer to a dialed-in audience = fewer touches to convert.

A weaker offer to a broader audience = more touches to convert.

More touches = spending more on advertising.

Think of your purchasing behaviors as a consumer.

When you see an ad for the first time, do you jump up and immediately book a service or pay for the product?

Probably not.

It usually takes several reminders about the brand or offer before we, as consumers, take action.

Now we know that we have to earn the trust of the customer. To do that we may have to serve them several advertisements or "touches" to get them to buy our offer.

So, how do we shortcut earning trust?

How do we cut the number of times we need to get our brand in front of a customer?

How do we shortcut this process when we have a grand opening coming up in a matter of weeks?

> **Essentially, how do we lower the barrier to purchasing?**
>
> **Answer: We create an offer so good the customer no longer feels hesitant to trust us and doesn't need to be reminded to take action.**

We have to create an offer so good the customer would feel dumb not taking advantage of it immediately.

How do we make an offer this irresistible and create fear of missing out?

We will break down various strategies you can use to craft an offer for your specific business. Keep in mind that every company, service, and product is different.

Think of the methods below as various options you can use together to build your offer.

This is called offer stacking.

> **Offer stacking is taking various strategies and tactics and layering them together. Doing this creates a single, irresistible offer.**

An example of stacking could be providing a discount for a limited time and pairing it with a giveaway for one lucky winner.

Another example could be a discount on a service or product only available to the first 100 people who buy. A bonus will also apply to each purchase. And last, everything comes with a 100% satisfaction guarantee.

Remember, you need to be able to look at the offer with zero bias and say to yourself, **"Wow, there is no way I would miss out on this. If I were my target customer, I would have to stop what I'm doing and buy this." If you don't say that to yourself, your offer is not strong enough.**

With that being said, here we go.

DISCOUNT PRICING

This is the most obvious and commonly used tactic. You are providing a heavy discount on an otherwise premium service or product that packs a ton of value.

> **But the discount has to be large enough to get people to stop what they are doing and take action.**

The amount that you choose to discount will depend on the price point of your product or service.

When giving a discount, we have found that providing a dollar amount (ex: $50 Off) is more impactful than a percentage (ex: 50% Off). A dollar amount is clear; a percentage amount requires the customer to do the math. We want to limit the amount of thinking and decision-making the potential customer has to do.

The easier we make it for someone the better.

If you offer a premium service or product, you likely don't want your brand to be known for discounting, and we agree. In this case, your advertisement should say this is a one-time offer, and you won't be providing a discount again. That will lend itself to the following two strategies - urgency and scarcity.

URGENCY

Urgency is a metric of time. Most grand openings will naturally involve urgency because they will only last a few days. Your immediate goals will dictate how long you want your grand opening and the offer to last. In our experience, 1-3 days produces the best results because it creates an urgency to act and a fear of missing out.

SCARCITY

Scarcity is a metric of available units. Communicating a limited number of units is a great way to promote urgency and fear of missing out. Once they're gone, they're gone.

BONUSES

Bonuses give you a lot of freedom to be creative. A bonus can be anything that doesn't usually come with your product or service. It can be something you usually upsell that you temporarily include for free; or it can be something you have never offered and are not planning to offer again.

It can be a BOGO (Buy One, Get One) or a collaboration with another business with the same customer base. It could be a free product. There are many options you can explore when you consider adding a bonus to your offer.

GUARANTEES

Guarantees can scare some business owners, and we understand why - no one wants to refund money. However, a 100% money-back guarantee increases trust and lowers the barrier to purchase.

Why? Because there is no risk to the customer.

Most people will not ask for a refund if you have a quality product or service. They will be happy with their experience. Therefore, you gain more by offering the guarantee and paying off the minority who take you up on it.

> **This is also a great strategy to decrease negative reviews.**

If someone doesn't love your product or service, they are less likely to post a negative review if they get their money back.

GIVEAWAYS

Who doesn't love winning prizes? We all do.

Giveaways are a great way to drive a lot of excitement within your audience. **The best thing about giveaways is that you can require specific actions to enter the giveaway in addition to buying your product or service**.

Some valuable actions are:

- 'Like' our Facebook page
- Follow us on Instagram or TikTok
- Tag two friends in the comments
- Share this post

These extra actions increase engagement, and some of them share your offer with your customer's friends and family for free. **This helps you gain more customers without increasing your acquisition costs**.

> The only mistake to watch out for is asking your customer to jump through too many hoops to enter your giveaway. We recommend requiring only 1-3 actions on the same platform to enter to win.

We've reviewed different strategies and tactics to build an FOMOGO offer.

Now, let's talk about the elephant in the room.

WHAT WILL A FOMOGO OFFER COST ME?

By now, you're probably thinking about your profit margins during your grand opening. This is especially true if you plan on discounting or giving away free products or services. But how much should you discount and give away?

Great question.

> **We believe that the benefits of providing an FOMOGO offer and an experience worth sharing will significantly outweigh the short-term loss on your initial profit margins.**

Especially if you plan it well.

F.O.M.O.G.O Offer Benefits > F.O.M.O.G.O Offer Costs

That is the mindset we encourage you to have.

Hear us out. When we do this we get the following:

- ☀ We will receive a lot of positive reviews all at once. This is great for future customers to see when deciding if they want to buy from us. It also helps our authority online, which helps our SEO.

- Customers will post about us. This spreads our brand to other similar audiences for free. This also helps as people's opinions and experiences carry more influence than paid advertising.
- We can build the start of a solid customer list which we know will help with future sales.
- Overall, we'll increase the likelihood of creating a business with a viral coefficient greater than
- We want this experience to be share-worthy. That is what we need to grow at a faster rate.
- If we can get a viral coefficient greater than 1, we will start to see customer acquisition costs decrease.

For example, Netflix offers a one-month trial of its services for free. That's a great offer that lowers the barrier to purchasing. It's easy to sign up for one month with no risk to the customer, and Netflix knows that. Even if it has to absorb the first month's costs, it will yield many profitable months to follow.

Netflix can do this because they are confident that your experience will be positive. You can follow a similar strategy for your business.

We hope this chapter highlights the long-term benefits of creating an FOMOGO offer.

Now that we have your offer ready, it's time to broadcast it to your potential customers.

Keep reading to learn how to advertise your offer effectively.

Action Steps:

1. Write down ideas for each element listed above.
2. Create your FOMOGO Offer by stacking various combinations of the elements together.
3. Write down at least 3-5 offers that you think your audience will have FOMO if they miss out on them.
4. Show those offers to people you personally know that fit your customer avatar and get their opinion about the offer.
5. Pick the one that gets the strongest feedback.

Chapter 10

Step 4: Traditional Marketing VS Digital Marketing

"We have technology, finally, that for the first time in human history allows people to really maintain rich connections with much larger numbers of people."

- Pierre Omidyar

You've come a long way, and the day is almost here! Your FOMOGO offer is complete, and it's time to start advertising it.

But before that, let's cover some differences between digital and traditional advertising. We'll also discuss which route gets most people more bang for their buck.

First, let's talk about traditional marketing methods. We're talking about offline methods. This can be print flyers, direct mail, billboards, radio, and television.

Printed flyers are costly and take a ton of effort to hand out. The time/money investment vs. reward may not be worth it. This depends on how you execute this strategy.

Direct mail may be a good idea, but there is no way of knowing whether your audience is reading your mail. Direct mail has a similar cost to handing out flyers, but you have the added component of postage costs.

This can be a viable strategy but not always the most efficient one. Beyond this, direct mail does not offer a lot of tracking or analytics. You can target demographics but have limited analytics. The best way of tracking results with direct mail is by advertising your FOMOGO offer and requiring the customer to bring that piece of mail in for redemption.

Billboards are expensive. With billboards, you have no analytics except the estimated daily impressions from drivers. So there's no way to know what demographic is seeing your ad.

Radio is also expensive compared to digital marketing. With radio, you know roughly who the listeners are. Still, you cannot track if they're paying attention when your radio ad is playing.

People listen to the radio during their commute. Because they are driving, they might not focus on the radio, nor are they in a position to write anything down. Radio ads have become less relevant over time with the rise of streaming platforms.

Television is also expensive compared to other methods of advertising. Your premiums can vary depending on when you play a particular ad. You have rough demographics, but people don't pay as much attention to commercials as they used to. In fact, most people reach for their phones and start scrolling when one comes on. Streaming platforms such as Hulu and Netflix have made traditional television less relevant.

With the rise of digital marketing, brands have more power over advertising effectiveness.

Digital marketing offers a lot more tracking and analytics. It allows you to trim more fat out of your advertising, get more results and waste less money.

You can see how many people are clicking on an ad.

There's visibility over how many people go past a particular advertisement stage.

You can see whether people book an appointment from an advertisement.

You can view where they abandon the process.

You can see the number of impressions you're getting, your reach, and more!

The data points go on and on.

In any case, we want to be clear. We're not saying that traditional methods don't work.

We're saying that often, you get more bang for your buck with digital marketing compared to the latter.

When every dollar in a grand opening counts, it's essential to know this and leverage it.

So why the big push for advertising your grand opening?

Simply put, **no one will know you're having it if you don't advertise it**.

There's a common saying that you should **dig the well before you're thirsty**, and that's what our ideology is.

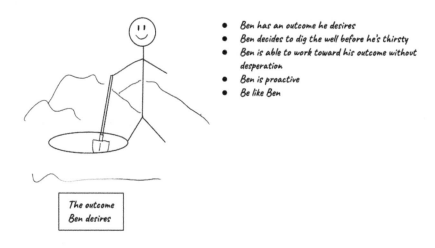

- Ben has an outcome he desires
- Ben decides to dig the well before he's thirsty
- Ben is able to work toward his outcome without desperation
- Ben is proactive
- Be like Ben

The outcome
Ben desires

We want so much pent-up demand that when you finally open, that demand comes rushing through like a flood. To get that flood, you want to use ads to build awareness, excitement, and demand for your business. You want it before opening your doors.

Keep reading to learn how we've done this successfully over and over again.

Action Steps:

1. Check your mail and see what brands still use traditional marketing.
    a. Take note of what they are offering.
    b. Do some brands have a more compelling offer? If so, why is that?
2. Take screenshots of the ads that get your attention online and ads with lots of engagement (shares, comments,

likes). Add these screenshots to a Google Slide and continue to do this as you see ads.

   a.   Take note of what they are offering.

This is called having a swipe file, and every good advertiser has one.

Chapter 11

Step 5: 7 Steps To Winning Grand Opening Ads

"Many a small thing has been made large by the right kind of advertising."

- Mark Twain

Social media has become a staple in the way customers interact with businesses online.

As a result, it is often one of the first things consumers check when evaluating a brand or business. But, it's important to note that most platforms have minimal organic reach.

Most brands on mainstream social media platforms have less than 2% reach. When brands have less reach, it incentivizes them to pay for advertising to reach more people.

Let's think about this.

If you have 2% reach and 100 people that like your page, only 2 of them might see your posts in their feed.

One thing brands can do to increase reach is to use hashtags. Hashtags are like labels that allow you to categorize your posts. This way, your post might show up if people search for or follow a specific hashtag.

Reach can increase over time by getting engagement. But it's hard to get engagement when you have minimal reach.

See how this works?

Some brands choose the organic route when it comes to building their following and business. This is an option, but it takes much more time than most companies have before opening.

You need customers now, not later. Paid advertisements allow you to get reach on your posts and your FOMOGO offer immediately.

Before you run ads, it's important to note the approach and mindset you should have. You want to squeeze the most juice (money) out of your ads and not have them squeeze the juice out of you.

You can approach advertising the same way that scientists run an experiment. When we test ads we only test one variable at a time. This ensures we get data that is clear to understand.

So what do we mean by this?

First, let's talk about the four main pieces of an advertisement.

Creative - the media we're showing in the advertisement. It could be a video or picture for example.

Copy - the actual words written on the advertisement.

Targeting - who you show the advertisement to.

Destination - where we send the traffic we target. This could be a form, landing page, website, etc.

If you wanted to determine which piece of creative out of a set of three was best, it doesn't make sense for those ads to have different versions of copy. You would want all of the other advertisement pieces to be identical.

Doing this ensures you get a clean sample of which creative works better because you are testing one variable simultaneously.

If we tested out more than one variable at a time, the data would not be clear. One of our ads could work, but we would not understand why. Testing one variable at a time is how we systematically ensure we get to winning ads over time.

So how do we start this process?

For this, we use our 7-step process.

> **Step 1** is deciding on your objective and goals.

> **Step 2** is researching your competitors, the market, your demographics and coming up with your FOMOGO offer.

> **Step 3** is to select your platforms, campaign type, timeline, and destination.

> **Step 4** is setting up your targeting. For targeting, use the consumer demographic we discussed in earlier chapters.

Step 5 is setting up your Scroll-Stopping Creative & Addictive Ad Copy (more on this later).

Step 6 is to create copy and creative variations, decide which variable you will test, install tracking, and publish the campaign.

Step 7 is to analyze and optimize your ad campaigns with additional testing and retargeting.

Let's talk about these a bit further.

Since you've made it this far into this book, we assume you're clear on your objective and goals. So let's keep moving forward.

Step 2 is doing your research.

This critical step can shortcut your learning curve and save you money. When we start our research, our first priority is to see what's already out there. We're trying to notice what gets engagement from the customers we want to attract.

But we want to be clear, we don't copy, and we don't want you to copy. That's plagiarism. The point is you want a good gauge of what people resonate with and what's already working in your market.

You can do this by looking at similar businesses that have successful advertising. Suppose you can't find suitable models for some reason. In that case, you can look at other businesses acquiring the same customer. Doing that works even if they sell a different product.

The point is to understand what's getting your market to respond. Following this process is a great way to gain insight into what resonates with your target demographic.

Let's move on to the next step.

Different platforms offer different advertising objectives. It's crucial to select the platforms that provide the objectives you're looking for and that have the audience you want to attract.

Step 3 is deciding on platforms, objectives, and your timeline.

We have found great success with Facebook, Instagram, and Google. The platform you choose can vary based on your audience.

After you select a platform, you have to choose your objectives within the platform.

Do you want landing page views, booked appointments, messages, online purchases, brand awareness, likes, phone calls, views, engagement, clicks, leads?

Different objectives, such as these, are available on various advertising platforms.

Our agency tends to use booked appointments, purchases, messages, landing page views, phone calls, brand awareness, engagement, and leads.

Now, when do you start running ads for your grand opening?

The timeline can definitely vary. Based on our experience, we have seen the best results around one and a half to two months before opening.

That's enough time to build up excitement and to pivot if any of your campaigns don't take off as well as you'd like them to. Anything too far in advance, and people forget about it. On the flip side, anything too late and it's hard to build up the necessary traffic. So our sweet spot we've found is about two months.

When you have less time than that, it requires you to be more aggressive with your ad budget. Less time also equals less margin for pivoting. But we'll talk more about ad budgets in a little bit.

From here, you need to decide the destination of where you will be sending traffic for your initial tests. Your destination can be your website, landing page, social media, messenger, lead form, phone, booking calendar, etc.

Remember that the destination should be specific to your grand opening. It can lead to fewer conversions if you have a general website and send people to that website. This is due to the number of distractions.

Regular websites have different tabs, blogs, and fields people can click. When those options are available, the chance of them booking for your grand opening decreases.

It's best practice to send traffic somewhere where the only action they can take is the action you want them to.

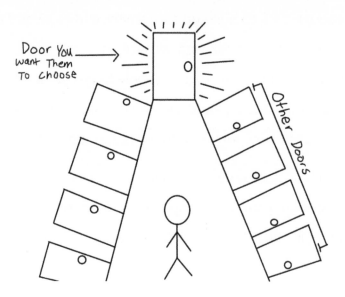

To drive this further, imagine you ask someone to walk down a hallway with doors on each side and one at the end.

If there are 20 doors in total, what is the likelihood that person will open the door you want? It's about a 1/20 chance, which aren't great odds. Your destination works the same way. So make sure that your destination has limited options the traffic can take.

Remember when we spoke about attention span?

Well, it applies here. Every dollar in your advertising budget counts. So it's important you're not wasting them.

> **Don't send people to destinations where they'll get distracted.**

Instead, we recommend choosing at least two destinations to test. Testing two variables when you start will help you learn which converts best. After that, you're ready to move on to the next step.

Step 4 is setting up your detailed targeting.

Setting this up should be easy. You already did the work of outlining your consumer demographic. Input it into the platform in the best way you can.

You want to try to create different segmentations of the same audience. This will give you different variables to test.

Suppose you are trying to attract people interested in hunting. In that case, you can segment other interests they might have into separate audiences. That way, you can know precisely which interests work better.

For example, let's say a hunter has an interest in the brand Real Tree and Smith & Wesson. You can test one audience with the Real Tree interest and another with the Smith & Wesson interest. Doing this will inform you which interest works best for your demographic.

Another example could be if you sell Jiu Jitsu gear. A person who does Jiu Jitsu may have an interest in brands like Venum or the IBJJF (International Brazilian Jiu Jitsu Federation). Targeting these interests would help ensure that your advertisement is seen by someone practicing Jiu Jitsu. This increases the likelihood of a purchase.

What you want to avoid is going too broad with interests. If you are trying to attract the attention of a mom, for example, just because a mom might like Starbucks doesn't mean you should add Starbucks as an interest in your targeting. Unless of course, you are trying to sell them coffee. This is because Starbucks is an interest that appeals to too many people and is not specific to moms.

Once your targeting is complete, it's time to move on to **Step 5: Scroll-Stopping Creative and Addictive Ad Copy.**

> **Scroll-Stopping Creative is creative that causes a pattern disruption in someone scrolling on their phone or computer. Scroll-Stopping Creative is critical because if someone doesn't notice your creative, they aren't going to click on or read your ad.**

Let's visualize this. A person is scrolling on their preferred social media platform. While they are scrolling, BOOM.

They see our ad and it stands out so much that they stop and read it. That is what we are trying to achieve when building creative.

> **We always start with the question, does this creative stop my scroll?**

Once you decide on what creatives you will use, it's wise first to show them to people that you know fit your target demographic for feedback.

See what they think, as this will give you some helpful insight on improvements you can make. But, you can't rely only on this because people you know aren't always the best reflection for the rest of the market.

So what are some other elements of Scroll-Stopping Creative?

We've found that reinforcing the offer in the creative boldly elicits a stronger response. We want the FOMOGO offer to be something that people can see at a glance almost immediately.

As a rule of thumb, the smaller the effort it takes for the consumer, the better. Remember, there's high demand for their attention, so their attention span is likely short.

People may skip over it if it isn't attractive enough.

At this point, you might be saying, "okay, this is great, but how do I make this kind of creative if I'm not a graphic designer?"

Fortunately, there are many different solutions you can use for creative. If you don't have these skills, Canva is one of the tools we recommend. It's effortless to use, free, and has a ton of tutorials you can watch.

Beyond that, Canva has a lot of templates and a drag-and-drop builder to make this easy for anyone.

Adobe Spark is another similar tool. There are many tools you can choose that are comparable. Don't get too hung up on which one you use. Just start creating.

What if you don't want to do it on your own or you're too busy?

No worries. There are other solutions for this too.

You just have to spend a little money to get it done. One of the easiest and best options is websites like Fiverr.com. Fiverr allows you to find professionals to do work for you for a reasonable fee. There are many people on Fiverr who specialize in creating ads. There are even people who specialize in ads for a specific platform.

Fiverr is especially easy because you can see samples of their work before hiring them. Fiverr also lists ratings and reviews, which is helpful. Seeing the reviews will give you peace of mind because you can see what you're getting before committing. Of course, this is not an exhaustive list, just some of the high-value and easy solutions we recommend.

At this point, it's time to start working on your Addictive Ad Copy.

We define Addictive Ad Copy as ad copy that entices your reader to read line by line and keeps hooking them in.

So how do we go about doing this?

It's first important to mention that **advertising copy has four main parts: a headline, a subheadline, a body copy, and the call-to-action.**

The **headline** is the first line of words your reader will see in your ads. A strong headline will hook the potential customer. It will compel them to read more about your products, services, or opening.

The **subheadline** is an extension of the headline and follows right after it.

The **body copy** contains the meat and potatoes of the advertisement. It focuses on explaining the details of your FOMOGO offer, and it is the primary text in your ad.

The **call-to-action** is the final piece of your ad that tells your readers what to do after viewing the ad. An example could be clicking a button to visit your website, going to a website to book an appointment, etc.

Now that we got that out of the way, let's discuss some of the things we've seen to help improve your ad copy. This way we can get the audience to read it.

We recommend addressing your audience immediately in your headline. Addressing them immediately will let them know it's applicable to them.

So if you're advertising towards dads, you could put, "Hey, Dads" in the headline. Another example is if you're trying to attract dads in a specific location. You could start the headline like this:

"Hey, dads in [Insert Location]"

Doing this will help ensure that the right people read your ad. The next thing we do is present the FOMOGO offer right after. That way, we have something strong enough to hook them. We often like to do this in question form. The question could address your audience's pain or a benefit they might want to receive.

For example:

"Hey [Insert Location], Dads, are you interested in getting rid of [insert pain point] for good?"

Or

"Hey [Insert Location] Dads, are you interested in getting [insert benefit or FOMOGO offer] during our Grand Opening?"

The subheadline expands on the headline and encourages them to keep reading. This part could also explain the FOMOGO offer or talk about benefits the reader might receive urging an action.

For example:

Headline: *"Hey [Insert Location] Dads, are you interested in getting [insert benefit or FOMOGO offer] during our Grand Opening?"*

Subheadline: *"If you said yes, then keep reading below!"*

Next up is your body copy. As we mentioned, your body copy will have all the details of your opening, business, service, and FOMOGO offer. Include the date ranges of the FOMOGO offer, whether there's a limited quantity, restrictions, an address if applicable, a phone number, and other vital details here.

Finally, your call to action will end your advertisement. It should be evident what you want your reader to do and how they should do it. We recommend reinforcing your offer here as well.

For example: *Book an appointment today by clicking the button below to get [insert FOMOGO offer]*

When this is complete, it's time to move to step 6.

Step 6 is to create variations of the copy and creative to test different combinations, decide on which variation to test first, install tracking, and publish your ads!

Making different variations is crucial so you have different ads to test should your initial test not produce the results you are looking for.

Creative variations can include the following:

- ☀ Different background colors

- ☀ Different animations

- ☀ Different placements that highlight the offer

- ☀ Video creative vs. Static creative (a photo or graphic)

Copy variations can include the following:

- ☀ Different headlines

- ☀ Different sub-headlines

- ☀ Different body copy

- ☀ Different call-to-actions

- ☀ Rearranging the order of the information listed

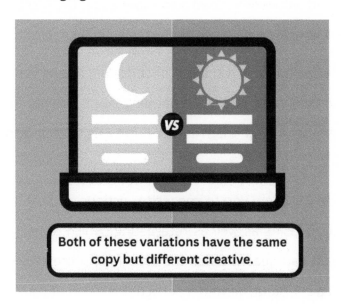

Both of these variations have the same copy but different creative.

Once you have the variations you want to try, it's time to pick your favorites as an initial test. But before you publish your ads, you need to install tracking.

> **The more complete end-to-end tracking you can set up, the better.**

End-to-end tracking refers to being able to see the moment someone starts interacting with your ad all the way to a confirmed purchase or completed action. This requires tracking codes from the platforms you use.

For example, if you wanted to see whether someone booked from an ad, you would need a tracking code. On Facebook, this is the Facebook pixel. Other platforms have their version of this.

The Facebook pixel is a snippet of code that allows you to track visitor actions on a website or landing page. You get that code from Facebook and then install it on your landing page or website.

This code will allow you to see visitor actions and use them for better advertising as well as retargeting (which we will get into later). You can see whether they made a successful booking, initiated a checkout, viewed a particular section of your website, abandoned cart, and more.

It is powerful.

To be successful you want to pull on the best levers you possibly can. Tracking helps you do that and know which levers to pull. It's vital to use whatever is available to you to maximize your effectiveness. When you maximize your effectiveness you stretch your advertising dollars.

One of the questions we get asked during this process is, **how much should someone spend on ads?**

Our answer depends on a variety of factors.

What is the price point of the service or product?

What is the LTV of a customer?

What is the average order for new customers?

Suppose you're offering something expensive and luxurious. In that case, you'll typically need a larger budget to acquire those customers. In most cases, this shouldn't be an issue. If something is expensive, there tends to be a high-profit margin.

> **As long as you are profitable, spend as much as possible to the capacity your business can handle.**

Let's say, for example, something that costs $20 per service. We have found great results running between $20 to $100 per day on Facebook with a similar ad spend on Google. We can scale up or down that number depending on how the ads perform.

We don't make concrete recommendations and say, "this is what you need to spend," because it does vary. Personal and business finances come into play here. Only you know what your business can afford.

From there, you're ready to publish your ads!

The various platforms are always changing their interface and processes, so for the purposes of this book we will not go into a step-by-step on how to launch ads. There are many YouTube resources available that can break this down for you.

After the ads run for a couple of days (we recommend 3-5 days), you want to see how well those results are producing.

Checking these results, optimizing your campaign, and retargeting is Step 7.

Start off by answering these questions.

Are you getting the outcomes you desire? At what cost?

Which ads are people responding to the most?

Which target audience is producing a cheaper result?

What are people saying?

Is there engagement?

How well is this working?

These are some questions you want to start asking yourself. After we determine which ads people are responding to, we start trimming the fat off the campaign.

Trimming the fat off the campaign consists of turning the low performers off. When we do this we can establish the best-yielding results as the control for further testing.

Once we have our control, we can produce more variations. Then we repeat the testing process to see if we can beat the control and establish a new control. This process is the scientific optimization approach we discussed.

The key thing to understand is that small adjustments over time equal massive gains.

There's a wise saying, **"what is not measured, does not grow,"** which is very applicable here.

To measure the success of your ads, you want to start going through analytics. Different platforms have different tracking dashboards and analytics for this purpose.

Depending on how deep you want to dive, there are many data points to track in marketing. But, in a general sense, we recommend the following.

First, you want to track the results you're getting for the objective you set. Depending on your chosen purpose, that will vary. You also want to measure the cost per result of that objective. That will give you insight into profitability.

Beyond that, here are other metrics to consider:

- ☀ The number of clicks you're getting, which are people clicking on your ad.
- ☀ The number of impressions and the cost you're getting them at.
- ☀ Your CPM is essential to measure, so you know how much it costs to show 1,000 impressions. This indicates how cheap your traffic is.
- ☀ Your reach so you can see how many people have seen your ad.

This is by no means an exhaustive list. We could do a deep dive into analytics but that is beyond the scope of this book.

Going further, it's great to follow up with your customers once they convert and ask them how they heard about you. Store this information to help you improve your future advertisements. This way, you have an idea of where your efforts produce more than others.

But, managing your expectations during this whole process is very important.

> **Just because you run an ad one time doesn't mean people will take action.**

That is extremely important for you to understand and accept. This is why retargeting is crucial for any campaign.

As we mentioned in an earlier chapter, there's a reason Coca-Cola continues to advertise to us. They need to stay top of mind, even though everyone knows who they are.

> **It takes multiple touches from a brand to get someone to convert.**

To put how often this happens in perspective, answer this question.

Have you ever Googled something and then out of nowhere you saw ads for that product or service everywhere?

Most of us feel like the internet is stalking us.

What is happening is that companies are retargeting us because we went to a website with a tracking code installed. Over time you see these ads enough, and your likelihood of buying increases.

We call this an external retargeting system. We use the term external because we are retargeting people that are outside our business. Meaning they have not converted.

Here's a bonus for after you gain a customer from advertising: an internal retargeting system is also essential.

Internal retargeting comes in the form of retention programs that get customers to keep coming back. You want to incentivize your customers to purchase more than once. Otherwise, when you acquire a new customer through advertising, you are essentially paying to replace the previous customer you lost.

An example of this could be a punch card program or giveaway for established customers. You can get creative with it. The main rule is selecting something good enough to incentivize them to keep coming back. You have options here. This system is part of continually winning their business.

> **Retargeting allows you to squeeze the most juice out of your ads instead of letting them squeeze it out of you.**

Here's a story to show you the impact of our 7 Step Process.

We followed this exact process with one of our clients not that long ago. Their grand opening was a huge hit. In fact, it went so well that their corporate office invited them to speak at a conference about it.

They wanted to know how they achieved their success. As a result of this process, we helped them break a franchise record. This game plan is the same process we've used to help scale other franchises and brands. We can tell you with confidence that **there's a formula to running successful ads. The best part? Any business can follow it.**

Now that we've covered how to get eyes on your opening, **keep reading to learn how you can get even more attention with instant trust.**

Action Step:

1. Work through and complete steps 1 - 7 of the above process. If you're not ready to run your ads yet, you can always leave them saved as a draft until you're ready for them to go live.

Chapter 12

Step 6: Getting Local

*"Alone we can do so little; together we
can do so much."*

- Helen Keller

What if you could save money by tapping into the audiences of local **businesses that are already serving your ideal customer**?

You can, and you should. This chapter is about leverage, one of the most important things you can have and build as a business owner. **In this instance, you are leveraging the work another business owner has already done**.

Leverage is power and there are ways to pull the levers around you to shortcut years of customer acquisition. You can do this by leaning on the trust built by other relevant businesses and influencers.

One of the most effective ways to market your business is with grassroots marketing.

Grassroots Marketing

But what is grassroots marketing?

> **Grassroots marketing targets a specific demographic that already has an interest in your business or niche.**

Let's take Moms, for example. Moms are customers of businesses that provide services for their children.

So let's say you own a dental practice that only works with children. It would make sense to partner with a similar business that provides children's services.

This could be a salon for kids, a pediatrician, a local indoor play zone, a children's boutique, a daycare, etc.

These businesses already serve the exact people you are trying to attract. If you can find a way to work with them, you'll immediately be able to tap into the customer base they have built.

There is another avenue you can explore, which is local influencers.

Influencers are the people you see online with a large following or audience.

People who follow influencers consume most of their content. They trust the influencer and are more likely to buy recommended products or services.

For example, as a consumer, you may get targeted by ads to try a new restaurant opening up in your city. The restaurant might seem like something you'd enjoy, but you're not in a rush and haven't thought about it.

What if a local influencer you trust posts about their great experience at the same restaurant?

You feel like you know this person. Their preferences are similar to yours because they're kind of like you. Maybe you've even purchased products or services they recommended.

Now, after seeing their post, you might be more excited to try the restaurant sooner than you had intended. The paid advertisements didn't convince you, but the influencer's post did.

You might have waited months to try that restaurant. And the restaurant would have spent more in advertising to get you to convert into a customer. But one post from an influencer may convince you to make a reservation next weekend.

That is the power of influencer marketing.

So let's pull each of these strategies apart so you can decide what works best for you and your business.

CROSS PROMOTIONS WITH OTHER BUSINESSES

The first rule of cross-promoting with another business is finding a win/win for each of you. It doesn't create a mutually beneficial relationship if only one is benefiting.

Here are some examples of how you can do this.

> During your grand opening, invite other businesses serving a similar audience to be vendors. For example, if you own a salon for kids, you might ask a children's boutique to have a pop-up sale during your grand opening. The children's boutique would post about their pop-up sale to their social media accounts during your grand opening. In turn, you would advertise the children's boutique as a featured vendor during your grand opening.

As a result, your salon would get exposure to the boutique's customers, and the boutique owner would get exposure to new customers attending your grand opening.

Leave behind flyers or business cards. It's very easy to make an agreement with another business to leave your flyers with each other. This allows each of your customers the opportunity to discover your business.

Use discounts or other incentives only available to customers of another, similar business. For example, a kid's salon could promote that when customers buy a haircut, they'll get a $10 gift card to the children's boutique. The children's boutique can promote a $5 off coupon to the kid's salon when they buy at the boutique.

You can also exchange social media posts that have the same effect. Both parties can agree to make a specific amount of posts about each other's business. To do this, you want to make sure that both parties tag each other in their posts so that way it's easy for the audiences to find the business.

> **There are many ways to get your brand in front of another similar business's audience. You just have to work to build a relationship with that business and find a way to make it beneficial for both parties.**

ONLINE GROUPS

Online groups, such as Facebook Groups, thrive on community. People are always looking for a tribe of people they can relate to. This is a biological instinct for most of us. Most of us want to share ideas and talk about similar topics of interest to other people. You can leverage this. **All you have to do is find these groups and learn how to work with them to promote your business**.

Communities can exist on various platforms, such as Reddit, online forums, Telegram, Discord Facebook, and more. But for the sake of simplicity, we will use Facebook as an example.

Here's how to find, join, and interact with these groups.

On Facebook, you'll want to search within Facebook Groups for groups related to your niche. In keeping with our same example, you can look for mom groups - they are very common.

If your business is local, you'll want to find groups for moms in your specific city. If your business is online, this won't matter as much.

Remember that every group has different 'rules,' so you'll likely have to request to join. Once you're in the group, you'll be able to start posting and commenting on other people's posts. **However, DO NOT immediately start pitching your business**. There are usually rules about promoting, which we will get into.

There may be times when you cannot join the group because you don't fit the demographic. For example, mom groups usually will not allow men to join. In that case, you will need to send a direct message to the group's admin to discuss your goals. You can also ask a trusted business partner or spouse to join the group on your behalf as an alternative.

Once in the group, you will want to learn the rules so you stay within them and don't get kicked out.

Once you've done that, message the group's admin privately and explain that you are a business owner. Then, ask how you might be able to promote the business within the group. **Depending on the group, these options might involve paying a fee or only posting on specific days**.

If they charge you a fee, the fee will be dependent on a few factors, and you will have to decide if it is valuable or not. We suggest looking at past posts to determine whether a group's advertising is worth paying for.

Did they get engagement?

Were members of the group commenting on the offers?

> **If you don't find evidence of engagement or support, move on to another group that has better results.**

Once you find a group you can post in, you'll make a graphic reflecting your business and the offer. This can easily be done on a platform such as Canva.com. You'll also provide ad copy to go along with it.

You can follow this formula in many groups of the same niche as your business.

LOCAL INFLUENCERS

Influencers exist on many platforms, including Instagram, YouTube, TikTok, and Facebook.

But be warned.

Not all "influencers" are created equal. What we mean by this is just because someone has a large following it doesn't mean they influence their following.

For example a Miami based influencer with 2.6 million followers wanted to launch a clothing line.

In order to get the manufacturer to agree to produce the line she had to initially sell 36 shirts. Unfortunately that influencer failed to do so and the clothing line never took off.

Why and how did this happen?

Truth be told, it could be for a variety of reasons.

That influencer might not have had an actual strong influence on her following. Perhaps the product didn't resonate with her following or the demand wasn't there. It could even be that she just didn't promote the products well enough.

Whatever the reasons were, you don't want to end up in the same position.

So how do you evaluate if an influencer actually influences and if they're a good fit?

Here are some things to consider.

First evaluate their brand as a whole.

How many followers do they have? This will be your primary indicator of whether they are an influencer. We hesitate to give you a number of followers to use as a baseline, but typically, a local influencer will have at least a few thousand followers.

Do they post regularly? If they are building their following, they are likely posting a few times per day.

Are they local to your area if you have a local business? Finding an influencer living in Florida doesn't make sense if your business is local to Phoenix.

Are their followers local?

Do they post about other local businesses?

Do they have a track record doing similar promotions to the one you'd like to do?

Do their followers engage with their content by leaving comments, 'liking' posts, and sharing their content?

Engagement is one of the biggest things you are looking for. It is better for someone to have 5,000 followers that are very engaged with their content, as opposed to someone with 10,000 followers with no one engaging.

Quality over quantity is important here.

Doing this research will save you money and time in the long run.

Once you have found an influencer, you will reach out as we did with the Facebook Group's admin.

Influencers usually monetize their platform, so they will likely be ready with options for you to choose from.

They may offer to visit your business and create a post or reel. You might be able to negotiate a complimentary service or product in exchange for their work. But we usually see this as a paid option.

> **Either way, our goal is to get them to create content that resonates with their audience.**

Our only warning with influencers is to be cautious of who you pick. **Pick another influencer if your business doesn't align with their audience**. Also, don't be afraid to ask them what kind of ROI they have gotten for previous businesses they have worked with.

Here are two tips on executing this strategy.

> **Tip 1**: Use one influencer or strategy at a time. If you have multiple influencers or businesses posting about you at the same time, it can be hard to see which of them is working best for you. The exception is if you are using a tracking system such as an affiliate code, which we recommend.

Tip 2: Don't overcomplicate starting the conversation. Many business owners ask us for scripts on how to communicate with these groups, businesses and influencers. We recommend keeping it simple. You are just starting a conversation.

For example, "Hey my name is <insert name> and I own <insert business>. I was interested in collaborating with you so I wanted to reach out. Let me know if we can make something happen.

Or

"Hey my name is <insert name> and I own <insert business>. We share the same audience. Interested in collaborating?"

This starts the conversation without you having to make an offer first and will allow that business or person to respond with what they typically do. The key thing is to find a win/win.

And that's it! You've done all the work, and customers are lining up for your business. It's almost grand opening day!

Keep reading to **make sure you squeeze as much juice out of your big day as possible**.

Action Steps:
1. Make a list of all of the following that are applicable to your business:

a. Local businesses you're not in competition with that share the same kind of customer base (audience).

b. Local influencers that deliver content to your customer avatar.

c. Online groups that have your customer avatar as community members.

2. Start reaching out to the influencers, owners of these businesses, and communities. Let them know that you are planning your grand opening and you would love to collaborate with them and get a deal in place.

Chapter 13

Step 7: Grand Opening Day

"The best way to predict the future is to create it."

- Peter Drucker

Your Grand Opening Day is here!

So, how do we make sure we create a great experience that your customers can't wait to share?

That's what we are going to cover in this chapter. **We'll talk about what you need to do to capitalize on all your hard work up to this point**.

This includes setting your team up for success and learning how to squeeze the most juice out of your grand opening as possible.

But before we dive into all that, I want to talk to you about the movie 'The Founder.'

The movie is about the McDonald brothers, who co-founded McDonald's. If you've never watched it, we suggest you do so before your Grand Opening Day, even if you only watch this one scene.

Early in the movie, the brothers are working to figure out the most efficient way to build the kitchen for the restaurant. Doing so gives them a fluid service model which results in excellent customer service and the fastest possible order delivery.

The scene opens up with the brothers standing on a tennis court with their employees. With chalk, the brothers draw an outline of a McDonald's kitchen on the court. They include all the appliances and stations. The grill, fryer, and even the condiment station are drawn.

Then, the employees would walk on the tennis court and simulate daily service based on their role. For example, the employee who manages the grill pretended to flip burgers. The employee who made the french fries pretended to fry them.

The staff continued to pretend to perform their roles on the tennis court within the boundaries drawn by the brothers. **They practiced their roles while the brothers figured out the inefficiencies**.

The brothers stopped the staff when they wanted to make a change.

They removed the employees from the tennis court and drew a new kitchen schematic. Then they had the employees rejoin them and rerun the simulation.

The brothers repeated this process until they had a harmonious flow. Then they had their kitchen custom-built to those exact specifications.

This ensured that right after a customer ordered within seconds they received their order.

This completely set McDonalds apart from the competition. You can do a version of this for your own business.

We're not telling you that you need to draw out the layout of your business on a tennis court unless you want to, of course.

However, this scene illustrates the importance of building efficient systems and setting high standards. Taking the time to do so results in a great customer experience and improved efficiency.

But, of course, it's one thing to train your employees to do a job and do it well. **It's another to get them to take ownership of the customer's experience**.

For example, does your team understand the customer's journey from beginning to end?

Do they know the role they play in that journey and the importance of it?

Where in the journey should upselling occur?

What scripts should they know, and do they know when to use each one?

When are we capturing the customer's information, and what are we capturing?

When are we asking the customer to leave us a review?

How are we getting customers to post about us to gain user-generated content? Why do we even need user-generated content?

Are we providing a membership? If so, when are we offering it?

What about a rewards system?

This might sound like a lot of planning, but you've put in a lot of work and money to get these customers. We want to turn them into long-term buyers, and we want them to share their experiences.

So, let's break each of these down.

CUSTOMER JOURNEY

The customer journey refers to all the interactions a person can have with your business. Typically, it starts the moment a customer hears about or experiences it. We want to choreograph this experience as much as we can.

Think about it like dining at an expensive restaurant.

1. You make the reservation online. The restaurant will ask for your name, email, and whether you are celebrating a special occasion.

2. A confirmation email pops up in your inbox confirming the date, time, and the number of guests.

3. You pull up, and the valet takes your car and parks it for you.

4. When you walk in, the host or hostess welcomes you warmly by name, smiling, and leads you to your table. Relaxing music plays in the background.

5. A team member brings water and bread.

6. The server welcomes you, recites the featured menu items, asks if anyone has allergies, and offers cocktails.

7. The cocktails are delivered quickly.

8. The server returns and asks if anyone would like to order an appetizer.

9. Your water is refilled without you having to ask.

10. The server makes intelligent recommendations for dinner when asked and suggests complimentary items.

11. Dinner arrives hot and perfectly presented; everyone's food arrives at the same time. The server has prepared the table with steak knives or additional utensils.

12. Used plates and utensils are removed from the table as needed.

13. The server removes crumbs from the table.

14. Hot towels are distributed.

15. Each guest gets a dessert menu.

16. Dessert arrives and "Happy Anniversary" is written on the plate because you indicated that it was your anniversary when you made the appointment.

17. The check arrives with the owner's business card in case feedback is necessary.

18. Paying the check is easy.

19. As you're walking out, servers and hosts wish you well and thank you for visiting them.

20. A team member asks to take your picture in front of the famous 'wall of wine' they are known for, which is perfectly lit.

21. The valet brings your car curbside, and you find a 'thank you' note in the cupholder.

22. The next day, you receive an email from the restaurant thanking you for coming in. It also asks you to leave a 5-star review if you had a great experience and an option to make your next reservation.

You want to think of your business in the same way.

Take some time and think about how you want your customers to feel. Then, think of actionable steps you can train your team to perform to create that feeling.

SCRIPTS

If you don't coach your team on what to say to your customers, they will decide for themselves. Failing to create scripts is the first step to a poor and inconsistent experience.

Here are some things you can write scripts for depending on your business:

- When a customer comes through the door
- When they approach the front desk or the first employee to assist them
- How to ask for necessary information such as name, email, phone, etc.
- How to describe what your business does or sells
- How to describe the products you sell
- How and when to upsell products or services
- What to say during the service or experience
- What to say to get customers to sample products
- How to confirm what the customer is asking for
- What to say at checkout or when paying
- How and when to ask for a review
- How and when to offer a membership program or loyalty program
- How to ask for user-generated content
- How to sign up for your newsletter and why they should

- How to pre-book them for their next service
- How to respond when a customer has a complaint or concern
- What to say when a customer asks for a refund

We're not trying to program the personality out of our staff, but providing an SOP (Standard Operating Procedure) full of scripts, what to say, what not to say, etc., can go a long way.

The trick to scripts is constantly improving them, especially when selling. For example, you might start with a script for upselling a product that you feel confident with. But once you start using the script, you discover that only a few people buy.

When that happens, you have to find a new approach or angle in your script to test.

Keep improving and refining your scripts until you get the customer to buy.

Now, even with the best scripts, you won't get the customer to buy every time. That's just not realistic. **But the goal is to track your conversion rates and improve them with each iteration of your scripts**.

UPSELLING

There is always an opportunity to increase your average order value (AOV). You'll know what this could be for your specific business. The goal is to determine when to present the upsell and what to say. If you can figure this out, you can train your team to include it in the customer journey every time.

You could upsell a bottle of wine for a restaurant when two people each order a single glass.

You could upsell add-ons like aroma therapy or extended foot massage for a massage studio.

For professional yard maintenance, you could upsell a driveway power wash at the end of the service so everything looks clean.

> **The perfect upsell is the next logical thing your customer will need to buy after they purchase your product.**

The first sale solves the first problem they have. The upsell solves the next problem created by the first sale.

For instance, imagine you own a yoga studio. You sign someone up for classes. One of the next logical things that they might need is a yoga mat. After they get a yoga mat, they may need a yoga block.

Upsells work best when designed in a funnel or sequence.

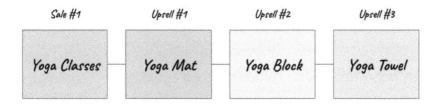

When you do this effectively, not only are you increasing your average order value, but you're providing more value and satisfaction to the customer. This makes them more likely to share your business and buy again.

TIP: When you increase your average order value, you can spend more on advertising to acquire new customers. If you have an average order value higher than your competition, you can outspend them. If you can outspend them, you can dominate your market.

INFO CAPTURE

Gathering or confirming personal customer information during the Grand Opening can be valuable. But before we move forward, let's talk about security and trust.

We should be respectful and responsible with information we collect from our customers. We can lose trust when we take information from clients and then spam them. It's even worse, if we use their information in a way that the customer didn't intend. An exchange of information for a service or product requires trust. So make sure you don't lose it.

As we've talked about, building your customer list in a format you own, not a third-party company, is essential.

This is an opportunity to add the client's information to:

- Your SMS text list
- Email newsletter
- VIP rewards club
- CRM (Customer Relationship Management software)
- and more.

Think of the lists or platforms above as a way to build a relationship with the customer, not only as a way to sell to them.

Use these personal means of communication to add value to their lives and build trust. For example, famous entrepreneur, Gary Vaynerchuk, has a book called "Jab, Jab, Jab, Right Hook." His book's title is his way of describing the relationship between anyone who is selling something and a buyer. **As the business, you should always 'Give, Give, Give,' first and then ask them to buy from you.**

Customers want to feel like the relationship isn't one-sided. They want to feel like a business is providing them with a ton of value, making buying easier.

Depending on your business and brand, there are many ways of doing this. You can provide:

- 'How To' videos
- Daily tips in an SMS thread
- Weekly motivational quotes
- Workout tips
- Recipes
- Recommended products that complement your own
- Blogs written by your company
- Promotions from complimentary businesses you trust and might be working with

> **Your customer list should be something you're always watering and nurturing. This helps you stay top of mind, so they instinctually come to you when it's time to buy.**

REVIEWS

How many times have you had a great experience with a company but did not leave a five-star review?

Like most people, you probably owe a few companies some reviews. Forgetting to leave a 5-star review is standard consumer behavior.

> **Getting a customer to leave a positive review takes more effort than a negative one.**

Effort For A Positive Review	Effort For A Negative Review
💪💪💪💪💪	💪

When customers have a negative experience, they can feel compelled to leave a negative review.

This is why it's important to ask every customer to leave us a five-star review if they had a great experience.

Usually, this will come at the end of the service or after they have purchased a product. We recommend weaving it into one of your scripts when the customer checks out.

A good idea is to incentivize this behavior. **Assume no one will do anything without there being something in it for them.**

One of the easiest ways to do this is to let the customer know that when they leave a positive review it enters them in your weekly or monthly giveaway. What you give away is up to you. Just make sure it has value to your customer.

In some cases or for specific periods, you might offer a gift or discount in exchange for the review.

We also recommend sending a follow-up email thanking the customer for their purchase. In that email, ask them to click a button or give them a link to leave a review.

As we discussed in an earlier chapter, reviews act as social proof, which is powerful. But getting the review is only the first step. The second step is responding to every review, not only the negative ones. This tells your customers that you care about them. It also helps your business gain authority in your market and increases your search engine rankings organically.

Customers are busy and distracted. Getting someone to stop what they are doing and leave a review can take a lot of work. That's why we recommend an on-the-spot incentive if they provide a five-star review immediately.

Our favorite place to drive reviews is Google because it boosts how often you appear in search results, but your business may have a different platform you prefer.

REWARD OR LOYALTY PROGRAM

> **A reward program is a simple retention tool that gives your customer a reason to continue buying from you instead of your competitors.**

A simple formula for a reward system is using a punch card system. An example of this could be, 'Buy 9 products or services and get the 10th free.' This can apply to all different types of businesses. For example:

- If you buy nine smoothies, coffees, acai bowls, etc., the 10th is free.
- You can provide a free upgrade for a premium service like a massage.
- You can offer a free gel polish upgrade for a nail salon.

Think creatively, and you can develop a reward system as a retention tool for your business.

As we've mentioned, you'll want to add this offer to one of your scripts and present it to the customer every time.

Reward or loyalty programs are an easy retention tool because they do not need money upfront like a membership program.

MEMBERSHIPS

Memberships are a great retention tool. But they require an investment, unlike a reward or loyalty program, so we want to ensure they are valuable.

Sometimes a business owner will build a membership program by multiplying the price by 12 months and then discounting it by a small amount. Then the business owner gets surprised when no one buys it.

It may take several attempts to create your membership offer. The only way to know if you're providing something your customers want is to build and test it. But it's worth going through the iterations to learn what works best.

> **Think of a membership plan as a method to buy your customer's loyalty and create predictable revenue.**

When a customer pays for your services or product in advance, they become an exclusive client. So make it worth their while.

Here are some examples of how to add value to a membership program, so it sells:

- Give a gift or service on their birthday.
- Include a discount on products or services.
- Include VIP scheduling availability.

- Include early access to buy new products or services.
- Include one or more free products when they sign up as a sign-on bonus.
- Include a monthly bonus.
- Add them to a VIP newsletter with premium content and offers.
- Include free swag (business-branded products like a t-shirt or water bottle) if your business has branding people want to wear.

You want the membership to be so valuable that it basically pays for itself multiple times over when compared to the price the customer would have paid if they didn't buy the membership.

Membership should feel like you're part of a premium club. **They're a VIP member of your business**. People should feel proud to be a part of it. When people belong to something they value, they tend to tell their friends.

Important Note: Keep in mind that most people won't use their membership to it's fullest extent. For example, if someone is a part of your membership and receives a free service every month, it doesn't mean that every person will use that free service. For those that don't, it's essentially free money for your business. On the flip side, if they do use it every month, congratulations! They enjoy your service and you bought their loyalty. Plus, they are probably your biggest fans and are sharing your business with their friends and family. This increases the viral coefficient we mentioned earlier.

USER-GENERATED CONTENT

It's natural for humans to want to show their friends and family the exciting things they are doing.

That's why we want to create an atmosphere that encourages your customers to take a photo and share. Doing so helps your brand reach more eyes for free.

So, how do you get customers to take pictures and post them?

- **Aesthetics**. People want pretty things to post. Make your product, packaging, and store beautiful; people will want to take pictures.
- **Step-and-Repeat**. Depending on your branding and what you do, this might work for you. For example, this will work better at a salon than at a hardware shop. You can order a step-and-repeat with your logo for a few hundred dollars. People will naturally take photos in front of it.
- **Make it part of the customer journey**. You know when you ride a roller coaster, the company takes your photo while you're mid-ride and then tries to sell it to you after? Take this concept and apply it to your business, but don't

try to sell it back to them. For example, after completing a service, you can make it part of the team member's script to say, "The next step is to take your photo in our <insert photogenic location in the store> and make sure you post it to social media and tag us!" You can make this even more effective by incentivizing it. Which brings us to the next point.

- ☀ **Create a promotion to enter customers in a giveaway** when they take a photo of your service or product. Part of the requirement is to post it to their social media account and tag your business.

And that's it.

At this point, we've executed the grand opening. Congrats!

But how can you duplicate this process again in the future?

What if you're reading this book because you already opened your business and never had a grand opening?

Or, what if your grand opening could have been better?

> **The good news is you can repeat these steps at any time in your business.**

You can apply the steps we've learned to gain the same benefits as if you had a grand opening game plan the first time.

Keep reading to learn this simple reframe that will help you apply this in any situation.

Action Steps:

1. Think through your customer journey and plot it on a flow chart.

2. Determine the best places in the journey for upsells, asking for a review, and getting user-generated content.

3. Write scripts for every scenario and objection you may encounter.

4. Train your staff on the customer journey and scripts.

Chapter 14

What To Do If You've Already Opened

"Our key to transforming anything lies in our ability to reframe it."

-Marianne Williamson

So far, we've covered many tactics and strategies for grand openings. But what do you do if you've already opened?

Obviously, a grand opening doesn't make the most sense in this situation. But, if you're in that situation, don't worry because you didn't waste your time. You can implement everything discussed in previous chapters with this one simple reframe.

Instead of throwing a grand opening, you can throw a customer appreciation event. We treat this event the same way we would a grand opening. All the prep is the same, and all the marketing steps are the same. Everything you read in the previous chapters applies. It's virtually the same thing. We are just naming it something else.

> **The beauty of a customer appreciation event is that it helps acquire a large number of customers in a short time frame. With these events, you can choose any date to do it, and it creates goodwill with your audience and community. Events such as this, also have built in urgency, since they are an actual event. They also create social engagement and buzz.**

The only thing that we would recommend is that you don't do it too often. We typically call this a "customer appreciation event" or a "customer appreciation party." The name will vary depending on the amenities and feel of the event.

If you don't want to do this, you have other options. You could reframe the event around your anniversary and celebrate that. We have done anniversary parties and events in the past with great success. When it comes to execution, the same things apply here. Implement all the previous steps, but be sure to tailor your creative, copy, and FOMOGO offer to the new name.

A cause-based event is also a great idea. A cause-based event could be a drive for charity. You can make this even more timely by selecting a relevant cause in your area at that specific time. This one is compelling because it emotionally invests your audience further. This is because it allows you to use more emotionally driven angles in the ad copy and creative. When it is cause-based, the stakes matter more.

Beyond this, you could also use holidays. Any holiday that you think is relevant enough can work for this reframe. There are many different holidays throughout the year. All you have to do is open up a calendar and look at what makes sense. With these reframes, you're looking for something to theme around that will excite your audience.

The timeframe of the FOMOGO offer and event should be like a grand opening. A very limited timeframe for people to opt-in increases the urgency. A limited-time offer is critical to having a good turnout. We have found that there is no sense of urgency if you're doing something for an entire month.

> **No sense of urgency translates to lower numbers. When people think they have a long time to do something, they procrastinate and take a long time to do it. Sometimes it never even gets done.**

That's human nature. So limiting this to a week at most is what we recommend. Most of the time, we prefer one to two days on the weekend. That way, most of your audience is free from work obligations.

Unless, of course, they are busy on the weekend. If that is the case, you'll want to plan around that. Anything more than a week for redemption, and we see results, attentiveness, and sense of urgency die off.

One of the other questions we get asked is, "how often can we do this?" It's wise only to do this once or twice a year. That frequency will preserve the potency of the offer. Anything more than that, and the event starts to lose its strength.

The most we would ever feel comfortable recommending is once a quarter. Still, even then, we are reluctant to do so. The problem is that people will wait for the event to visit your business if you start doing it four times a year or more. Them falling into this pattern is not a good thing for your business. So resist the temptation to do this too much.

Let's talk about a story to show you the impact of this reframe and how this worked very well for one of our clients.

This client purchased a business that was already open. However, the company had negative reviews, staff issues, and problems with quality fulfillment. Overall the business was not in a great spot. Revenue had started declining because of the issues, but the company had potential. When our client took ownership of it, they began to understand the gravity of the situation. They needed a great way to turn it around and get a clean slate.

We encouraged the client to look at the negative feedback and address and fix those issues. After all, if we acquired more customers but the experience was the same, we would ruin the business's reputation even more. This would make any future events harder to do. After the problems were solved, we launched an event.

We let everyone in the local area know that the business was under new ownership. In the ad, we explained that they were throwing a customer appreciation event to thank all their past customers. This event also invited new customers to come to try the new experience.

The event was a massive success.

It created a lot of positive momentum and goodwill in the community. The locals talked and referred their friends and family to the business. This simple reframe allowed the business to start over. It was almost an instant turnaround. Using these reframes acts almost like a reset button on the business, but you must use them wisely. Otherwise, this will do more damage than good.

What's the takeaway here?

There are ways to implement these strategies when a grand opening doesn't go well, the business isn't doing well, or when you want to acquire customers in a short time frame.

You only have to follow this one simple reframe.

Now that we've set you up for success with your grand opening or event, keep reading to save yourself some pain.

In the next chapter, we discuss what crucial mistakes you want to avoid in this entire process.

Action Steps:

1. Brainstorm and write down how you would like to present the event you are planning.

2. Think about what amenities the event should have based on its theme.

3. Set a date and get started.

Chapter 15

What Not To Do

*"Smart people learn from their mistakes.
But the real sharp ones learn from the
mistakes of others."*

- Brandon Mull, Fablehaven

Congratulations, you're almost done!

You've put in all the work and laid out a great foundation. You have invested time, money, energy, sweat, and maybe even tears.

With all that investment, we want to ensure this goes as well as possible. With that said, there are some mistakes that we want to go over that could derail your effort.

So we decided to list them in this chapter to prevent you from making them. That way, you can be as successful as you possibly can.

First, let's talk about how mistakes can impact something with positive forward momentum.

> **Doing things wrong has a greater negative impact than the positive impact of doing things right.**

Read that again.

We see this in many areas of life, not just in business but all human affairs.

Humans are biologically programmed to pay more attention to negative things than positive ones. This is because, in the wild negative things can end your life.

There's a reason why the news tends to be more negative than positive. It's because negativity gets a stronger emotional response.

People are far more likely to share something negative than something positive. We see this all the time.

> **Psychologically people move more quickly away from pain than they move toward pleasure.**

Think about it. You are more likely to move if there is a fire in your house rather than an ice cream truck outside.

> **If you do something wrong, it is more likely that someone will share it than if you do something right.**

Think about this from your own experience.

Has there ever been a time you had an excellent experience, but you didn't share it, and you didn't leave a review?

Why was that?

For most of us, it's because we don't think to do so, or it takes more effort than we want. Now think about a time you had a bad experience. Did you share it? If you're like most people, you probably did to some capacity.

Even if you didn't leave a negative review, you might have told friends or family. The lesson here is that **just because someone has a positive experience doesn't mean they're going to share it. However, they likely will if it is negative**.

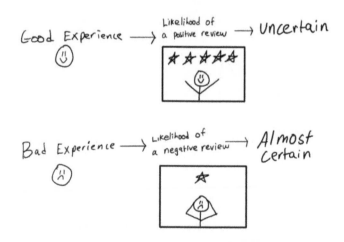

Knowing this is important to mitigate as many negative occurrences as possible. Too many negative situations could stop your business from growing.

Now that we've covered that, let's get into some of the mistakes you want to avoid.

Generally, you don't want to do anything with higher costs than returns.

We talked about this in other chapters when we mentioned LTV and CPA, but this applies to more than that.

We've seen this happen with billboards, other print media, and radio. We're not saying these things don't work, but it really depends on the situation. We see it as a higher risk.

The next thing you want to avoid is rushing your event and not allowing for enough time to advertise. What's the point of an event if no one attends it or not enough people know about it?

We've seen this happen more than once. It causes stress for the business owner because everything is happening too fast. **When there isn't enough time to advertise, your margin for error gets smaller.**

Ultimately, this leads to trying to dig your well when you're dehydrated. Advertising time can make or break the success of an opening. We recommend that if you're cutting it too close, it may be worth moving the date of your opening or event.

For example, you could do a soft opening before to get your feet wet and bring in some revenue. Then you can plan the event for a later date. That way, you have enough time to build up the traffic.

Another thing that you want to avoid is valuing short-term profit over the customer experience. This kind of thinking hurts you in the long run. **The customer experience creates revenue, forward momentum, and volume.**

What do we mean by this?

For example, suppose someone leaves you a negative review, and you disagree with it. In that case, it is not wise to argue publicly or at all.

Suppose you feel their motivation is to get something for free, and it's not warranted. In that example, it is best not to value profit over their customer experience. **When a customer tells people about their negative experience and leaves a negative review, it costs you more than it costs to make them happy.**

Negative Review	Make Them Happy
Cost: $ $ $ $ $	Cost: $

The best practice is to address it publicly once, and then move the conversation offline. You can do this by commenting on the review, addressing the situation, and explain how you would like to rectify it. **The biggest thing to do is show you care**. Then, other people can see what kind of business owner you are and how you value your customers. This takes little effort and goes a long way.

Here are some simple steps to doing this.

How to respond to a negative review (even if the customer is wrong)

1. Acknowledge their feelings.
2. Apologize for their experience.
3. Address their concerns by showing empathy.
4. Tell them that you'd like to correct the situation regardless of what it is.
5. Tell them to email you at your email, leaving the email address in the response.
6. Go above and beyond to make them happy.
7. Ask them if they'd kindly change their review after they are happy.

Example: Hi there. My name is <INSERT NAME> and I'm the owner of <INSERT BUSINESS NAME>. We apologize that you did *not have the <INSERT BUSINESS NAME> experience you expected. We care about each person that visits our business and want to make sure you leave happy and satisfied with your experience. Please email us at <INSERT BUSINESS EMAIL> so we can ensure we make this right.*

The last thing we want you to avoid is skipping steps in the processes outlined in this book. **When you alter a successful formula's variables, its results become unpredictable. Some machines have parts that have to work together simultaneously, or they don't work at all.**

These are some things we find important and want you to avoid. We've covered a lot of essential strategies and tactics up until now. Implementing them may be intimidating. But, **when faced with a difficult task, think about why you're doing it in the first place**. This will give you strength and motivation. Think back to your "why" and remember the success stories we discussed earlier.

You may just be the next one.

> **You're only one event away from changing your business and life. Keep reading, so we can wrap all of this up and go over what's next.**

Action Steps:

1. Evaluate whether you are making any of the mistakes listed in this chapter.

2. If you are, create an action plan to correct those issues.

Chapter 16

Conclusion

"That's all, folks!"

- Porky Pig

Congratulations, you did it! *cue confetti*

You've gone through every step of the Grand Opening Game Plan! You're now ready to plan an incredible grand opening for your business.

We wrote this book to help business owners understand the positive, long-term effects of having a great grand opening. We hope we have done that for you here.

Success is a result of an equation that can be broken down and followed. That's why we laid out the formula we have seen work hundreds of times.

As you've now read, there are a lot of steps to having a great grand opening. We recommend going back through this book and following it step by step as you plan your grand opening.

Remember, this formula can be learned and executed by anyone who wants to understand and put it in place.

Here it is again for convenience:

Foundation —> Audience —> Offer —> Advertise —> Local Grassroots = Appointments

You got this!

FREE GIFT!

So, what's next?

We hope we over-delivered and you got tons of value from this book.

If you need help applying what you've learned or have more questions, go to

www.almostmagicalmarketing.com

or scan the QR code below to schedule a free strategy session with our marketing agency.

LEAVE US A REVIEW!

If this book helped you achieve great grand opening results, please leave us a five-star review on the platform where you purchased this book.

We love hearing about your wins; it helps us get the word out so others can have the grand opening their business deserves.

FOLLOW US!

Heather Cutler

On Instagram @theheathercutler

Kris Olivo

On Instagram @thekrisolivo

Final Action Steps:

1. Pat yourself on the back; most people don't read books, let alone finish them!

2. If you found this book helpful, please leave us a review on the platform you purchased from. We will love you forever, so thank you in advance!

3. Follow us and let us know how this helped you. We love to share your stories with others.

4. Get to work and go be successful!

5. **FREE BONUS:** As a gift for finishing this book, visit this link or scan the QR code below for free bonuses!

    https://linktr.ee/almostmagicalmarketing

Sources

https://techjury.net/blog/how-much-time-does-the-average-american-spend-on-their-phone/#gref

The average mobile phone user checks their phone up to 63 times daily.

(Source: Slick Text)

https://www.slicktext.com/blog/2019/10/smartphone-addiction-statistics/#:~:text=The%20average%20smartphone%20user%20checks,notifications%20can%20contribute%20to%20ADD.

Americans spend an average screen time of 5.4 hours on their mobile phones daily.

(Source: ZD Net)

https://www.zdnet.com/article/americans-spend-far-more-time-on-their-smartphones-than-they-think/

Ingram Content Group UK Ltd.
Milton Keynes UK
UKHW011829160323
418676UK00004B/195